ORCHIDS
as
HOUSEPLANTS

ORCHIDS
as
HOUSEPLANTS

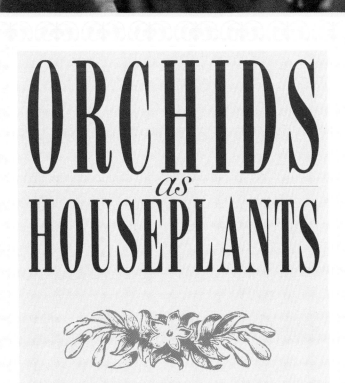

BRIAN AND WILMA
RITTERSHAUSEN

WARD LOCK LIMITED · LONDON

F4086—Orchids as Houseplants—Prelims—

First published in Great Britain in 1989
by Ward Lock Limited, Artillery House,
Artillery Row, London SW1P 1RT,
a Cassell Company

House editor Denis Ingram
Text filmset in Baskerville
by MS Filmsetting Limited, Frome, Somerset
Printed and bound in Portugal by Resopal

British Library Cataloguing in Publication Data
Rittershausen, Brian
  Orchids as houseplants.
  1. Indoor plants: Orchids. Cultivation
  I. Title   II. Rittershausen, Wilma
  035.9′3415

ISBN 0-7063-6815-0

CONTENTS

INTRODUCTION

We have written this book in response to the ever growing demand for basic information from those who wish to grow a few orchids without having the considerable outlay of purchasing a greenhouse, special equipment, etc. While many orchid enthusiasts become totally captivated by their plants and have an insatiable approach to increasing the size of their collection, others are content to grow orchids in a very small way, with just a few plants of their choice in the home. It is to these latter that we dedicate this book. However, we cannot accept responsibility for the 'orchid bug' taking over, and 'just a few orchids' becoming more and more in number, because this is what often happens. Because orchids are so very different, it is all too easy to fall under their spell and then there is not room enough on the chosen windowsill to accommodate all the orchids you would like to have. For this reason our book goes on to describe further methods that may be used within the home, which are still within the capabilities of the small indoor grower, catering for an ever-increasing and varied collection of orchids.

Before that stage is reached, if indeed it is, we hope our readers will enjoy this brief glimpse into the fascinating and beautiful world of orchids. We have mentioned but a very few from a vast and varied family of plants. But these few will introduce you to a completely new world and could change your life.

The complexities of pseudobulbs and aerial roots are explained, along with all the other factors which make orchids different from other plants.

There are as many different ways to grow orchids as there are orchid growers and everyone eventually finds the best way that works for them. Therefore opinions vary and advice differs. We have described the methods which have worked for us during our combined 75 years of experience, during which time we have repeatedly updated our ideas and improved our growing knowledge.

Orchids have given us a lifetime of pleasurable pursuit, friendships, and not a few surprises. One of us (Brian) has travelled the world in that pursuit, and we have both gained much satisfaction from our long association with the world's most aristocratic members of the plant kingdom.

We hope our readers will gain the same enjoyment and experience the same delights with their orchids.

B. R. & W. R.

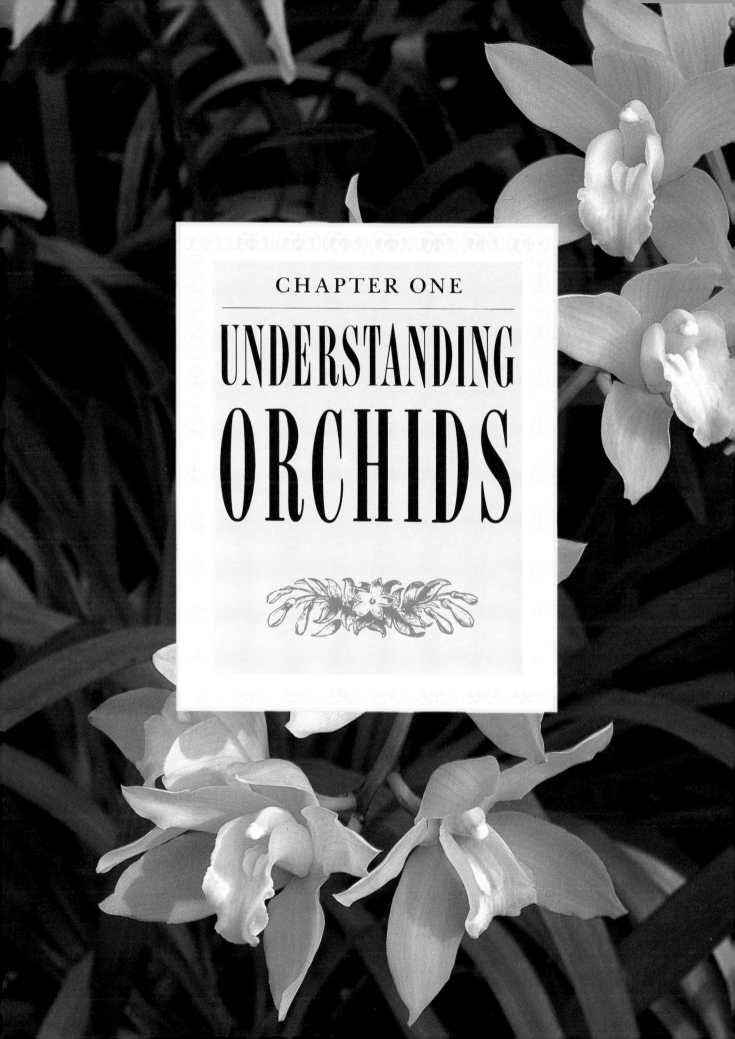

CHAPTER ONE

UNDERSTANDING
ORCHIDS

From the many thousands of tropical and temperate orchids that exist in the world, including the 25,000 or so naturally occurring species, a mere handful are suitable for growing indoors. Even this 'handful' gives the grower a wider range of plants to grow than in any other plant family, so great is its diversity and variety. Most are hybrids, although a few species are still available for the enthusiast, as the beginner will gain more satisfaction from the generally more rewarding hybrids.

The next chapter deals in detail with the various – and varied – species and hybrids which are happy growing indoors, but it is worth looking first at the component parts common to all orchids discussed in this book, as in some ways they differ radically from most other houseplants.

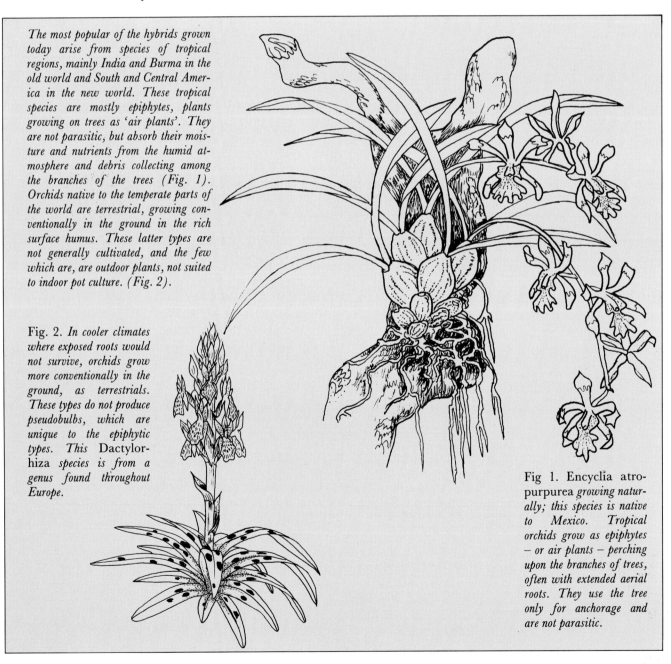

The most popular of the hybrids grown today arise from species of tropical regions, mainly India and Burma in the old world and South and Central America in the new world. These tropical species are mostly epiphytes, plants growing on trees as 'air plants'. They are not parasitic, but absorb their moisture and nutrients from the humid atmosphere and debris collecting among the branches of the trees (Fig. 1). Orchids native to the temperate parts of the world are terrestrial, growing conventionally in the ground in the rich surface humus. These latter types are not generally cultivated, and the few which are, are outdoor plants, not suited to indoor pot culture. (Fig. 2).

Fig. 2. *In cooler climates where exposed roots would not survive, orchids grow more conventionally in the ground, as terrestrials. These types do not produce pseudobulbs, which are unique to the epiphytic types. This Dactylorhiza species is from a genus found throughout Europe.*

Fig 1. Encyclia atropurpurea *growing naturally; this species is native to Mexico. Tropical orchids grow as epiphytes – or air plants – perching upon the branches of trees, often with extended aerial roots. They use the tree only for anchorage and are not parasitic.*

Fig. 3. *Flower shapes vary enormously, but all conform to a basic pattern. The orchid flower has an outer whorl of three sepals, which in orchids resemble the petals. An inner whorl consists of three petals. The third petal (at the centre) has been modified and is known as the lip or labellum. This is designed to attract the pollinator. The specific colouring at the centre of the lip is known as the 'honey guide'. Above the lip is a central column which contains the stigma and pollen. In orchids this is in a solid form held beneath the pollen cap or anther.*

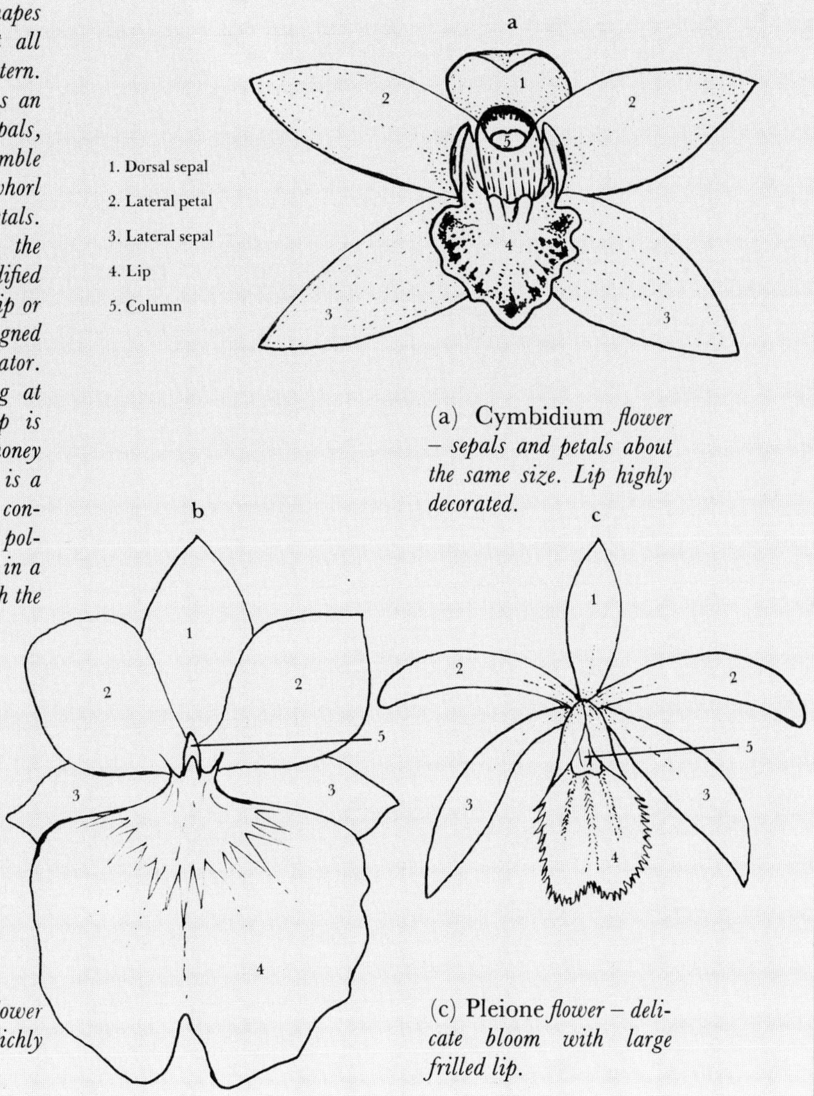

1. Dorsal sepal
2. Lateral petal
3. Lateral sepal
4. Lip
5. Column

(a) Cymbidium *flower – sepals and petals about the same size. Lip highly decorated.*

(b) Miltoniopsis *flower – lip very large and richly coloured.*

(c) Pleione *flower – delicate bloom with large frilled lip.*

FLOWERS

The blooms of orchids are different from any other flower, and it is their structure which sets orchids apart from all other plants. Because the orchid family is so very large and widespread, there is a tremendous diversity to be found among the flowers (Fig. 3). Even so, they all conform to one basic pattern which is then modified over and over again. Every orchid flower consists of three outer sepals, and three inner petals. Two are lateral petals and the third, varying greatly from the rest of the flower, is the lip or labellum. In paphiopedilums and their allied genera it is formed into a pouch. The lip is beautifully designed to attract the insect pollinator and provide a landing platform and 'honey guide'. This is achieved in some orchids in remarkable ways.

The sepals and petals surround the central structure, the column, which contains the stigma and stamens within. The pollen is held in small solid masses of yellow under the pollen cap or sited at the tip of the column.

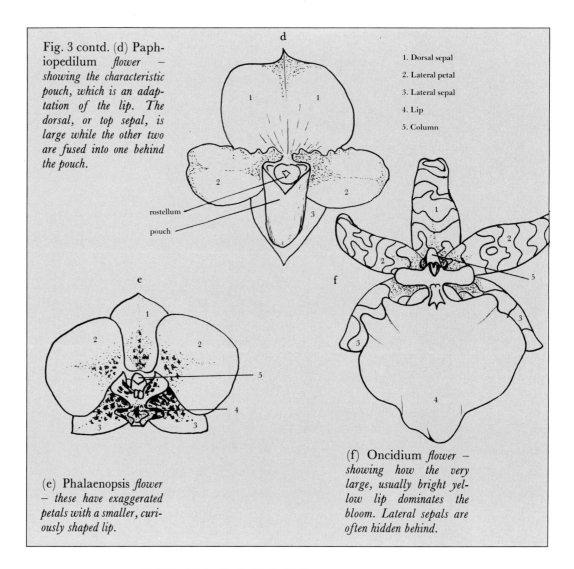

Fig. 3 contd. (d) Paph-
iopedilum *flower –
showing the characteristic
pouch, which is an adap-
tation of the lip. The
dorsal, or top sepal, is
large while the other two
are fused into one behind
the pouch.*

1. Dorsal sepal
2. Lateral petal
3. Lateral sepal
4. Lip
5. Column

rostellum

pouch

(e) Phalaenopsis *flower
– these have exaggerated
petals with a smaller, curiously shaped lip.*

(f) Oncidium *flower –
showing how the very
large, usually bright yellow lip dominates the
bloom. Lateral sepals are
often hidden behind.*

PSEUDOBULBS

Most, but not all, orchids in cultivation are epiphytes, and the majority
of these produce pseudobulbs. These are swollen stems used by the plant
for water retention. Pseudobulbs sit on the surface of the compost and
are so called because they are not really bulbs at all. The true bulb is of
course like the daffodil or onion which remains under the surface of the
ground. When a true bulb is cut vertically in half it can be seen to be
made up of layers of tightly packed embryo leaves. The inside of a
pseudobulb, on the contrary, resembles a potato, comprising closely
knit fibres capable of holding a considerable amount of water, which if
necessary can last the plant for several months.

Pseudobulbs are the toughest and most long lived part of the plant.
Likened to a tree which sheds its leaves while the branches and trunk
remain alive to support the leaves in another season, so the pseudobulbs
outlive roots and leaves. The first pseudobulb which starts a continual
succession starts its life as a small green protocorm which has swelled
from a minute seed. From it, the young leaves grow steadily while the
base gradually swells over a period of six to nine months to form the first
seedling pseudobulb. When mature at about twelve months, a com-

pletely new growth will start from its base. This will develop in the same way, slowly swelling through its growing season until it also matures, supporting its own leaves and roots. This second pseudobulb will be larger than the first, and so the progression will continue until by the third or fourth the plant has attained that magical stage of flowering. Now the latest and largest pseudobulb will commence flowering, a feat only possible in its first or second year of existence, depending upon the type. Also depending on the genus of orchid, the flower spike may appear from the base, as is the case with cymbidiums; from inside the first side leaf, as with the *Odontoglossum* types; or from between the leaves at the top of the pseudobulbs, as with *Cattleya* types and encyclias. Having attained flowering size, it is normal for the plant to bloom each year, as each new pseudobulb is completed or 'made up'. As new pseudobulbs are added, each one is an independent structure, yet all dependent to some extent on each other and joined by a rhizome. This is usually unseen and below the compost, although on the cattleyas and some encyclias it is visible, showing as a thickened woody bridge between the pseudobulbs. After a few years, usually from two to five, the oldest pseudobulbs will begin to show signs of age, the naturally plump exterior becoming wrinkled or shrivelled. As part of the natural ageing process the leaves will turn yellow and fall. On some pseudobulbs there is left behind a dead protective sheathing. On cymbidiums it can appear as if the leaves have been cut off at the base, but this is the natural appearance once the leaves have been shed. As the leaves drop with age, so also will the roots die back naturally, while the pseudobulb lives on, now in a dormant state. However, this dormant pseudobulb, having supported the younger ones for several seasons, will now become surplus to the plant's requirements, If left on the plant it will contribute little to its well-being, and eventually wither and die, but if removed it will start to grow from one of its dormant eyes around the base. The readiness of pseudobulbs to propagate in this way depends upon the genus of orchid.

The habit of growth described here is sympodial, where an entire new section of growth is added to the plant each year. Bulbless orchids, such as the paphiopedilums, are also sympodial.

The shape and size of pseudobulbs will vary with each orchid, some of the smallest (sophronitis, some maxillarias, erias etc.) may be less than 1 cm ($\frac{1}{2}$ in) high, while giants of over 2 m (6 ft) (such as *Grammatophyllum speciosum*) also occur. However, among the cultivated orchids they are mostly between 5 and 30 cm (2–12 in). Their shape may be round, (cymbidiums), oval (*Odontoglossum* types) or oblong (*Cattleya* types); shiny green (coelogynes) or clothed in protective sheaths (cymbidiums). The youngest are always extremely good-looking, and to watch them develop over the season is in itself one of the great thrills of orchid growing. The ageing process dulls and wrinkles them, but during the growing season they should look plump and 'full'. Some shrivelling during or just after the resting period can naturally occur, to be made up by the plant a few weeks later.

Little harm can befall pseudobulbs because they are the toughest part of the plant. If some calamity should occur, it is often the pseudobulbs which survive the leaves and roots, and through them the plant has another chance of regaining its health and strength. Pseudobulbs can be eaten by slugs and snails, fortunately not prevalent indoors as they would be in a greenhouse, so this need not be a problem for the indoor grower. Rots can happen for no apparent reason, usually in the winter months, which need to be treated with sulphur, and insects pests such as the various types of scale and mealy bug will find a home around them. Pseudobulbs which are aged and dying will be found to be soft and either brown or yellow in colour. At this stage they should be removed in case rot starts, which could spread into the living pseudobulbs. A soft and rotting pseudobulb anywhere on the plant should be removed for the same reason.

To recap, an orchid should show a good progression of pseudobulbs gaining in size until maturity is reached. If the size of the pseudobulbs has been reducing – that is, if the older, possibly leafless pseudobulbs are larger than the latest ones at the front – the plant is not progressing, and may be incapable of flowering in this state.

LEAVES

The leaves of orchids are as varied and different as it is possible to get, yet at the same time they are all basicaly the same! Supported by the pseudobulbs of the sympodial orchids they vary in number from a single leaf (pleiones) to perhaps eight or ten (cymbidiums). They can vary in length from less than 1 cm ($\frac{1}{2}$ in) to over 1 m (3 ft), the average being between 22 and 30 cm (9–12 in). They may be wide and oval (lycastes) or long and narrowly oval (zygopetalums). Their texture also is variable and can be related to their life span. Orchids can be evergreen or deciduous, so some leaves, such as those of pleiones, are designed to last one growing season only before being discarded, while others will remain on the plant for several years, becoming marked and spotted with age (as with *Odontoglossum* and *Cattleya* types).

Orchids which are not sympodial and so do not produce separate individual growths are called monopodial. These types, which include phalaenopsis, vandas, aerides and others, produce new leaves from a central growing point on an ever-extending vertical rhizome. While the vandas become taller by this habit of growth, adding leaves as they grow towards a maximum height, the phalaenopsis tend to shed leaves at the same rate as they produce new ones, therefore remaining always about the same size, with between three and six leaves at any time.

The first sign of new growth commencing is the emergence of a young leaf or leaves at the base (on sympodials) or centre (on monopodials) of the plant. Their progress to maturity is something to be watched and enjoyed. The leaves of pleiones, one per pseudobulb, are paper thin and among the shortest lived: initially protecting the young flower bud, within six months they will have grown and matured before turning yellow and dying before the winter. Lycastes, thunias and some dendrobiums will also hold their foliage for one season only, shedding it either at the end of the growing season (autumn) or at the start of the growing season (early spring).

Cymbidiums and *Odontoglossum* and *Cattleya* types retain their foliage for several years, losing a leaf at a time, again autumn or spring time. While dramatic, and sudden total leaf loss can be a natural occurrence for the deciduous types, should it occur with an evergreen type like cymbidiums something would be very wrong and the plant could be suffering from severe stress of some kind.

Leaves can tell you much about the health of your plant. Ideally, they should be a healthy shade of green, not necessarily *dark* green, as the colour will vary as does everything with orchids! So we say, a *healthy* green. Sickly yellow can indicate too much light, not normally a problem indoors; under-feeding caused by too infrequent repotting; or merely, as already mentioned, old age. A *dark* green can indicate too little light, often a factor which prevents flowering. Leaves will also change colour with the seasons, reacting to the amount of light available at different times of the year. During the summer, odontoglossums in particular will take on a reddish tinge to their leaves – this is a 'sun tan' and is to the good, but it is an indication that the plant is getting as much light as it can stand, any more and it could result in sun *burn*. This will show up as ugly black patches on the portion of the leaf directly facing the sun.

Leaves which live for several years become spotted and marked with age, often their tips will turn black or brown, a dead portion which may slowly extend down the leaf. These dead tips, to which cymbidiums are prone, can be trimmed off. If these or similar marks occur on any new growth, it may be cause for concern, a stress signal from the plant, and the culture may need closely looking into.

Old leaves dying naturally can be cut from the plant using a sterilized tool, or left until they drop. The latter avoids any damage to the plant, and prevents virus disease from being transmitted to others by using the same knife. Virus diseases which can attack orchids will show mostly in the leaves (see page 87).

ROOTS

The first thing you notice about roots is that they are noticeable! As often as not an orchid will have some of its roots hanging over the edge of the pot, clearly visible and a great source of worry to the beginner not yet familiar with this habit. The fact that orchid roots have a tendency, even a desire, to get out of the pot into the air is a reminder that these plants are epiphytic in origin. Ephiphytic plants grow on trees, using their strong roots not only to seek out food and moisture, but also as a means of holding on to their perch.

The importance of good roots cannot be emphasized enough: a true saying is 'no roots – no plant'. The roots of epiphytic orchids look and behave differently from those of other plants and it is helpful to become accustomed to them. Coming to terms with orchid roots and understanding the way they work for the plant is in itself a great step forward in orchid culture.

All orchids produce roots. They vary from genus to genus and plant to plant. Some produce copious mats of long dense roots (oncidiums, maxillarias) while others make do with a few spindly ones rarely growing more than 10 cm (4 in) long (coelogynes, epigeneiums). The roots are white or whitish, and consist of a wiry central thread surrounded by fleshy tissue encased in an outer spongy covering which is the velamen. The growing tip of the root is green, or occasionally pinkish, when active but becomes completely covered by the advancing velamen when the plant is resting. The roots of paphiopedilums are slightly different: they are brown and are covered in minute hairs, while other orchid roots are smooth.

Compared with other plants which are similarly long lived, orchids make fewer roots. This accounts for the beginner thinking their newly acquired plants are underpotted. Do not make the mistake of immediately putting them into larger pots. With sympodial orchids the life span of a root system is directly related to the life of the foliage above. As already mentioned, while the pseudobulb will go on living the leaves and roots die naturally after a few seasons.

A new root system will commence some time after the start of the new growth. The observant grower will look for them at the base of the new growth when it is a few centimetres high. Again the start of the roots depends upon the variety of orchid. Initially, small swellings, not always visible because they are beneath the compost, will appear at the base of the new growth to extend quite rapidly, either entering the compost immediately, as do cymbidiums and odontoglossums, or growing across the surface before either penetrating the compost near the edge of the pot (cattleyas, encyclias etc.) or growing over the rim. Provided the orchid is potted correctly in an open and well-drained compost, the roots will follow the inside edge of the pot gradually working their way down to the bottom, a sure indication that the compost is to their liking. Roots with the strongest tendencies will sample the compost then proceed to grow *outside* the pot in their natural fashion.

Roots made outside the pot are true aerial roots, and their appearance differs from those made in the pot. Although both are basically the same, the velamen is tougher and dryer on aerial roots, thereby affording some protection, and the growing tip is greener. They cannot become pot roots, and if potted will suffocate. In the same way, pot roots would wilt and die if exposed to the air. Whether the plant has aerial roots or pot roots they both behave in the same way, absorbing moisture and nutrients through the spongy velamen to be taken up into the plant. The aerial roots may be hanging free or attached to any available surface. In their natural state those roots which find their way into humus or debris would gather additional nutrients. Even so, these extra minerals are few compared with those taken up by the more conventional terrestrial plants. For this reason orchids can be considered weak feeders, and this should be borne in mind when artificial feeding is given.

The roots of monopodial orchids are even more inclined to be totally aerial. They grow from the lower part of the stem in vandas and allied orchids, often well out of reach of the compost. Phalaenopsis roots, in particular, adhere very firmly indeed to any surface they come into contact with. Their roots are especially attractive, being fleshy, silvery coloured with a pinkish growing tip.

Live roots are, as stated, white (except for paphiopedilums, which are brown), with or without a growing tip depending upon whether the plant is resting or growing. They can be very brittle and are easily snapped or damaged, and exposed tips are particularly vulnerable. If damaged they will heal and the root will regrow from higher up. Dead roots are easily distinguishable. The outer covering will have turned brown and will pull away leaving the inner core. Roots which have died naturally from old age will be withered and completely dried out. Any which have been prematurely killed, possibly by over-watering in the pot, will be found to be full of water, black and sodden, while roots suffering from prolonged dryness will be limp and dehydrated.

To summarize, roots cannot always be seen, but their health can be determined to the experienced eye, by observation of the pseudobulbs and leaves. If you are worried about the health of any plant, carefully remove it from its pot and examine the root ball. Without exception the reason for the plant's ill-health will be found here!

CHAPTER TWO

SOME ORCHIDS TO GROW

*I*n this chapter, we take a look at a few of the orchids within the most popular genera. These are by no means the only orchid types which can be grown indoors, but they are those which you are most likely to find in an orchid nursery or mail order catalogue, and they will give the beginner some idea of where to start among this vast family of plants.

THE MAIN GENERA AND VARIETIES

CATTLEYA *AND ALLIED HYBRIDS*

Cattleyas are tropical orchids which originate from the jungles of Central and South America. Their distribution covers an area from Mexico in the north, through Guatemala, Colombia and Ecuador to Peru in the south and includes the forests of Venezuela and Brazil. Many of the most important and showy flowers come from the last two countries.

Their habit of growth is unusual and their pseudobulbs are quite unlike any other orchid, being long and club-shaped with the narrow

Fig. 4. Cattleya *type hybrids produce large plants with club shaped pseudobulbs and large, frilly flowers* (a). *Smaller types produce brightly coloured flowers of a different shape* (b).

part at the base. Each pseudobulb carries either one or two thick leathery leaves and in the wild the plants are found growing in enormous clumps consisting of hundreds of pseudobulbs, each of which lives for many years. These great masses grow epiphytically, high on the branches of the host trees, and they can be in danger of crashing to the ground should the branch break under the huge weight. In cultivation these plants more usually consist of five to eight pseudobulbs per plant, at which size they are easily manageable. The pseudobulbs are joined to each other by a thick woody rhizome which sits on top of the compost and is clearly visible, unlike other orchids where the rhizome is underground and unnoticed. The flowering sheaths are produced from the apex of the completed pseudobulb. The sheath protects the buds at the earliest stage of their development until they literally burst out and open within a few days, generally during the spring or autumn months. Usually two or three large blooms – up to 13 cm (5 in) across – are produced from a single pseudobulb. These wonderfully flamboyant flowers are among the largest of the cultivated orchids (Fig. 4a).

The *Cattleya* species fall into two distinct groups: plants with one leaf per pseudobulb (unifoliates) and plants with two leaves of equal size on each pseudobulb (bifoliate). Although the flowering habits of the two types are similar, the unifoliates produce much larger, more showy flowers. The bifoliates are noted for producing many more blooms per stem, which, although smaller in size, lack none of the exotic beauty of their larger cousins and are often more richly coloured. The unifoliate flowers come in colours ranging from white through lavender to deep mauve with a few yellow strains, while the bifoliates range from white through pink to deep copper shades with yellow and green incorporated. The colour ranges have become intermingled through hybridization and have been greatly extended by further breeding with a number of closely related genera.

As with the odontoglossums, a number of new man-made genera have been developed which incorporate the qualities of the originals. The cattleyas are also in the same position as the South American odontoglossums and their allies, with very few found in cultivation today because the plants have become scarce in the wild and are no longer imported on a regular basis. However, for the purpose of the indoor grower, the hybrids are far more showy and rewarding to grow anyway, being more tolerant and easily catered for.

Laelia

Closely related and similar in appearance to the cattleyas are the laelias. This genus comes from the same parts of the world as the cattleyas and is very variable in habit and appearance. It is the Brazilian varieties which have become the most important in hybridization with cattleyas. The cross produces the genus *Laeliocattleya* and combines the qualities of the two genera.

While it is true to say that the hybrids within this group provide extremely robust plants which have a wide tolerance, making them most suitable for indoor growing, there are, nevertheless, two *Laelia* species which are worth growing. *L. anceps* and *L. gouldiana* both originate from Mexico where they are accustomed to a dry and sunny climate. Their blooms are carried on tall stems with up to four or five flowers being produced at the top. *L. gouldiana* produces a cylindrical pseudobulb with two pointed leaves at the apex, from between which

Laelia anceps. *One to four rosy pink flowers are produced in the winter from a long flower spike which comes from the top of the completed pseudobulb.*

grows a flower spike about 50 cm (18 in) long. The flowers are a rich rosy purple with a deeper purple lip. This plant has been a favourite with orchid lovers since early times and blooms regularly in the autumn. *L. anceps* has a similar habit of growth, but produces a single leaf from a more club-shaped pseudobulb. Its flowers are slightly smaller and are coloured a soft delicate shade of rosy pink. The lip is marked with deep mauve.

Sophronitis

Another important genus closely related to the cattleyas is the very small and compact Brazilian *Sophronitis* with its deep red flowers. While the cattleyas and laelias number many species in their groups, *Sophronitis* is an extremely small genus with less than half a dozen species. Of these, *S. cernua* and *S. rosea* are collectors' items which belong in the greenhouse of the more experienced grower. Due to their small stature and particular watering requirements they are not suited to indoor growing where the drier atmosphere is not conducive to their good health. The most noteworthy of this small genus is *S. coccinea* (Fig. 4*b*). The whole plant barely exceeds 5 cm (2 in) in height and consists of small, slender or roundish pseudobulbs topped with a single leaf. The flowers are produced usually singly, or occasionally two, on a short stem from the apex of the pseudobulb. Unlike the cattleyas and a number of the laelias, the sophronitis do not produce flowering sheaths; the buds emerge directly from the pseudobulb.

While this beautiful little species is widely grown in cool greenhouse collections for its own undeniable beauty, its hybrids have added much to its related genera. *S. coccinea* has been crossed with *Cattleya* to produce the genus *Sophrocattleya*, and with *Laelia* to produce *Sophrolaelia*, while a further step forward incorporates all three genera in *Sophrolaeliocattleya*. While these are the most well-known genera incorporating *Sophronitis*, they are by no means all that is available. The main influence of *Sophronitis* in these crosses has been to reduce the plant to a more compact and manageable size, easily accommodated on the window sill, and to add the brilliant red colouring found in the species. While most of the hybrids produce smaller flowers, they are often produced in abundance, while their brilliant colour outshines all other hybrids within this group. Although the majority of hybrids containing *Sophronitis* produces a multitude of red shades, other colours have come through, with orange and yellow being represented where different breeding lines have been used.

Brassavola

There is a further important genus which has also contributed greatly to the multigeneric hybrids within this group and, as with *Sophronitis*, it is mainly one single species which has been used for its breeding value. The genus *Brassavola*, which has a similar natural distribution to the above genera, contains many beautiful species, most of which are coloured a very light green. Of these, one species in particular, *Brassavola digbyana*, is outstanding in its flower and breeding qualities. *B. digbyana* is now correctly known as *Rhyncholaelia digbyana*, but for registration purposes involving hybrids the older name has been retained to avoid confusion.

The habit of this species is similar to the related genera, although the plant is slightly smaller in stature than the cattleyas, the pseudobulbs are slender and carry a solitary thick leaf, and the whole plant has a blue green colour. The species is considered to be very free-flowering in sunny parts of the world, but in Britain it is often shy in flowering due to the lack of the sufficient light for part of the year. It is best suited to a sunny greenhouse and is not recommended for indoor growing for this reason. A single large bloom is produced which opens to the most delicate green without trace of another colour. The most outstanding feature of the flower is the very large, rounded and deeply frilled lip.

This frill is found in no other species within this sub-tribe, and seldom met with in orchids at all. Its purpose is not immediately apparent, although it obviously has a function. While there are very few hybrids within this genus, it has been crossed with the aforementioned cattleyas etc., producing the *Brassocattleya* and *Brassolaeliocattleya* hybrids. To these hybrids *Brassavola* has added size, the shape of the lip and, where it has been most predominant, some beautiful pastel shades. Unfortunately, the deep fimbriation of the lip has never been reproduced in any of the hybrids to the same degree.

In addition to those already mentioned, there are a number of other genera within the same sub-tribe which will interbreed with each other and which produce even more complex hybrids. These are not so widely grown, nor so easily cultivated, and hence only mentioned in passing.

Choosing a *Cattleya* Hybrid

When purchasing a *Cattleya* hybrid it may be more satisfactory to ask for the specific colour you require unless you are reading from a catalogue, so numerous are the hybrids. From the pure-bred cattleyas the colour choice is mainly mauves, with perfectly shaped flowers as large as a plate. The best white hybrids, such as have been produced along the Bow Bells line of breeding, give a perfectly balanced flower of the purest white with yellow in the centre. Where the Brazilian cattleyas and laelias have been intercrossed, some of the most striking results have been large yellow flowers with purple or magenta lips, sometimes deeply veined in the throat with a rich gold. When the small, bright red flowers of *Sophronitis coccinea* are mixed with the blood of laelias and cattleyas the result is some of the most vivid colours to be found in the orchid family. One of the most popular and easy to grow among these hybrids is *Sophrolaeliocattleya* Jewel Box. It blooms regularly and never becomes too large. As with odontoglossums and cymbidiums, this group of orchids is easily mass-produced by meristem culture, a technique by which many identical plants are artifically produced from one clone, and excellent named varieties are readily available. Meristem culture is also know as 'cloning'. With so much interbreeding it has become difficult to generalize on the size of these hybrids as they can vary considerably. As a guide, the pure *Cattleya* and mixed *Brassolaeliocattleya* hybrids will require 20–30 cm (8–12 in) pots when mature, whereas those hybrids with *Sophronitis* or *Laelia* in their make-up are smaller.

So successful have these hybrids proved to be as houseplants, they are now widely grown throughout the world. They are quite happy in warm conditions, especially the slightly drier atmosphere prevalent within the house. However, they can grow too large for the narrow window sill and would be better suited to the sun lounge which will enable them to receive all the light they require to bloom well.

The multigeneric hybrids within this group nearly all rest for several months at a time. This resting period varies and may not always coincide with winter but commences when the plant has completed one pseudobulb, and finishes when that pseudobulb has flowered. While growing, the *Cattleya* hybrids can be given considerable applications of water and regular feeding to maintain their fast rate of growth. Both should be lessened as the pseudobulb nears completion and discontinued when development is complete and flowering imminent. After flowering, the new growth should be watched for. When it appears from the base of the plant, normal watering can be resumed.

Opposite: Sophro-laeliocattleya *Jewel Box 'Dark Waters'. This is one of the smaller growing* Cattleya *hybrids, more easily accommodated on a well lit and warm window sill. The wonderfully bright colouring is amongst the most vibrant of all orchids.*

COELOGYNE

Coelogyne is a large genus of orchids, of which only a very few species are obtainable and desirable for indoor culture. The main colour to be found among these plants is white, but there is such a variety in size of flowers and lip markings that the following recommended varieties could all be grown without duplicating the same features.

Coelogynes are widely distributed in the wild, with the majority of the cultivated species coming from India. The plants grow as epiphytes and thrive in massive clumps, some several feet across, consisting of up to a hundred pseudobulbs. The plants vary in size depending upon the species, but all produce handsome plants, with highly polished pseudobulbs topped by a pair of dark green leaves. Some varieties produce an abundance of roots while others seem to make do with just a few spindly roots, just sufficient to hold their anchorage on a tree. Most of the species have a growing season followed by a resting period, during which time in cultivation they are left completely dry. The flowers appear from the apex of the leading pseudobulb in some species, or from inside the new growth while it is still very young. More rarely, they are produced from the base of the previously completed pseudobulb. A few varieties produce a flower spike which will bloom in successive years; when one season's blooms have finished, the stem remains green until the following year when more buds appear from the continuously growing tip. None of these species produces branched spikes, and few of them are very tall.

Only the species are grown to any extent in collections; the few hybrids which have been produced over the years are very rare and sought after. The easiest varieties to grow in the house are among the species. They are recommended for their ease of culture, which if correctly adhered to will reward the grower with a dazzling display of blooms in the spring. The following species are neat and compact growers, and can be easily accommodated on a window sill or wherever there is limited space available. However, it must be remembered that these species require winter light if they are to bloom successfully the following spring.

Coelogyne ochracea (Fig. 5a) is the most delightful of orchids and appears to have everything for the home grower. The plant is neat and compact; it can be grown in an 8 cm (3 in) container, and stands about 23 cm (9 in) high in its pot. When the plant has completed its resting period, the new growth commences in the early part of the new year. The flower spikes appear from inside the new growth while it is still quite young and up to a dozen small, delightfully fragrant flowers are produced in the spring. These are a pure crystalline white, with the lip prettily marked in yellow and orange, and will last for about three weeks. Several new growths are usually produced in one season so several flowering spikes can be expected. Within a few years the plant will have doubled in size, and can be retained as a specimen, never becoming too large not to be easily handled, or can be divided to retain the small pot size, according to the space available.

A similar and equally desirable species is *C. corymbosa*. This plant is slightly smaller that *C. ochracea*, and the pseudobulbs a little rounder. The flowers appear slightly earlier in the spring, and last a good three weeks. Again, it is a species which readily produces several new growths each year and can grow quite large, but can easily be divided. The flowers are larger than *C. ochracea* with fewer carried on the sprays,

Opposite: *The yellow* Cattleya *hybrids show the lovely striking combination with the crimson lip. These plants have two flowering seasons, autumn and spring. Plants may bloom in one or both seasons each year. Flowers will last up to three weeks.*

23

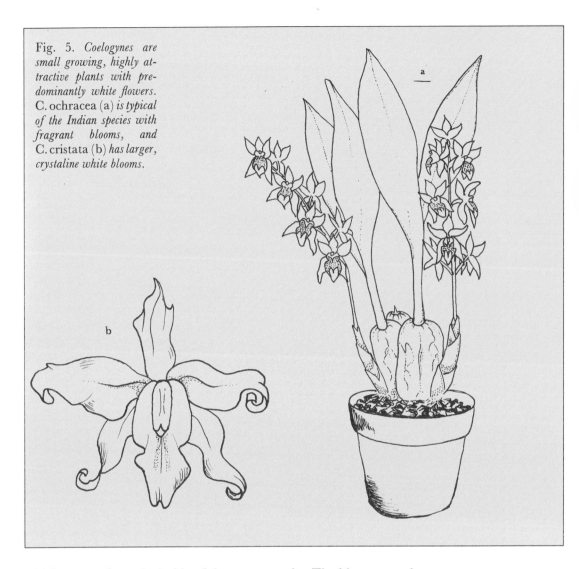

Fig. 5. *Coelogynes are small growing, highly attractive plants with predominantly white flowers. C. ochracea (a) is typical of the Indian species with fragrant blooms, and C. cristata (b) has larger, crystaline white blooms.*

which appear from the inside of the new growths. The blooms are the same crystalline white, but the lip is beautifully patterned with orange and brown markings. This handsome little plant can be covered in blooms when grown to perfection. It lacks the sweet fragrance of *C. ochracea.*

A further white species is *C. cristata*, which has been recommended for indoor growing since the earliest days of orchid cultivation. Enormous plants, up to 60 cm (2 ft) across, are sometimes seen, which have been grown on window sills for many years and appear to be totally neglected, often growing in small pots so crammed with pseudobulbs that the new ones have to be produced on top of the older ones. However, it is in this state that the plant thrives, and provided it is given all the light it requires, even to the extent of placing it out of doors during the summer months, it will reward the grower with a mass of showy white flowers in the spring. These blooms appear on short flowering stems which grow from the base of the previous season's pseudobulb. *C. cristata* (Fig. 5*b*) is the largest flowered of the recommended species, and the only colouring is the deep yellow stain in the throat. It is an extremely beautiful species, often called the 'rag orchid', a term which apparently refers to the ragged appearance of the

Coelogyne cristata. *A very showy species which can become very large if left undivided for a number of years. An untidy grower, it is happy trailing over the edge of its pot.*

petals which curl and crinkle, breaking up their outline.

While many other coelogynes are available, the above species are those which will succeed best indoors, coping better than others with the drier atmosphere. Some varieties can become extremely large, particularly the warmer growing species, which are not recommended. These are space-consuming and require much light for most of the year. As their blooms are short-lived, they give a poor return for the space they occupy in the home.

The watering requirements for coelogynes are similar to those for dendrobiums. The plants should be amply watered throughout the spring and summer while they are in active growth, to ensure the completion of good-sized pseudobulbs. During this time they can be lightly fed, and sprayed from overhead if possible. During the winter they enjoy a complete rest and should remain as dry as possible, avoiding too much shrivelling of the pseudobulbs, although a little shrivelling is a good thing and will improve their flowering performance the following spring.

Watering should commence as soon as the new growths are seen to be moving. This is particularly important with *C. ochracea*. If this species is kept too dry while in young growth, the leaves may become covered with a sticky substance which, if not washed off, can impede the development of the young growth and flower spike inside it. A curious feature occurs with *C. cristata* when the buds are near to opening. At this stage they turn brownish with a wrinkled, unhealthy look which can cause concern to the grower. This appearance is natural and within a couple of days the buds will open to reveal the full beauty of the blooms.

CYMBIDIUM

Cymbidiums, like so many orchids, are widely distributed in the wild. They occur in an area of the Far East which stretches from the Himalayas, across southern China and the southern islands of Japan, and down through the East Indies to the northern territories of Australia. Most of the species are of botanical interest only, with small, insignificant flowers. Also among the cymbidiums is an unusual subter-restrial species, a minute plant which produces small flowers on a short spike about 8 cm (3 in) high. None of these more obscure species has qualities which make them useful for breeding purposes.

Cymbidium Flame Hawk. Still the most popular of all the orchids in cultivation. This red-flowered hybrid is a typical modern 'compact' variety. Blooms will last up to eight weeks. Flowering period, winter/spring.

Cymbidium *Valya Craig*. The 'Standard' cymbidiums are space-consuming and need sufficient room to grow. Most suitable for a sun lounge with plenty of headroom and good light, which is important for them to flower well.

A typical cymbidium from which the bulk of hybrids has been raised produces egg-shaped pseudobulbs completely covered by the leaves. These leaves are up to 1 m (3 ft) long and there are eight to ten per pseudobulb. As is typical of orchids, cymbidiums grow in enormous clumps in the wild, but in cultivation are maintained at a convenient size: a large plant will consist of eight to ten pseudobulbs in a 30 cm (12 in) pot. The hybrids have been produced mainly from species which grow at high altitudes in cool, airy forests either as terrestrials where the soil is well-drained, or as epiphytes growing in the forks of large trees where there is space for them to expand into large clumps.

In cultivation the hybrids produce their flowering spikes during the late summer from the base of the latest completed pseudobulb, These spikes grow continuously for six months or more before opening their blooms on long stems during the winter and spring months. The spikes may be 1 m (3 ft) long with anything up to twenty blooms, depending upon the variety, in a range of colours from the soft pastel shades of pink and white, yellow and green, to the rich reds and bronzes. The lip is white or cream and heavily or lightly coloured around the edge. This colouring varies from the most delicate spotting, to heavy, all over blotching, barred with crimson. The flowers are amongst the longest lasting of all orchids; eight to ten weeks in perfection is not unusual. They have become the most popular cut flower with the florist and the blooms can commonly be seen for sale in shop windows, usually as individual blooms in cellophane packs.

Cymbidiums are the largest of the cultivated orchids and can become very space-consuming. For this reason they are not the most suitable for growing on a window sill or in a small room. Requiring space in which to grow and plenty of air and light, they are ideally suited to the garden room or sun lounge.

The *Cymbidium* hybrids can be divided into two types: the standard or largest varieties (Fig. 6a), and the miniatures (Figs. 6 *b* and *c*) which have been bred along different lines to produce a much smaller plant. These miniature cymbidiums are better suited to the window sill and can be obtained in the same range of colours as the larger varieties. While in the standard varieties the hybridizer has strived to produce a bigger bloom, the miniatures have been bred to retain the same qualities in a more compact shape and size. They have therefore become very successful plants with both the home grower and with owners of small greenhouses.

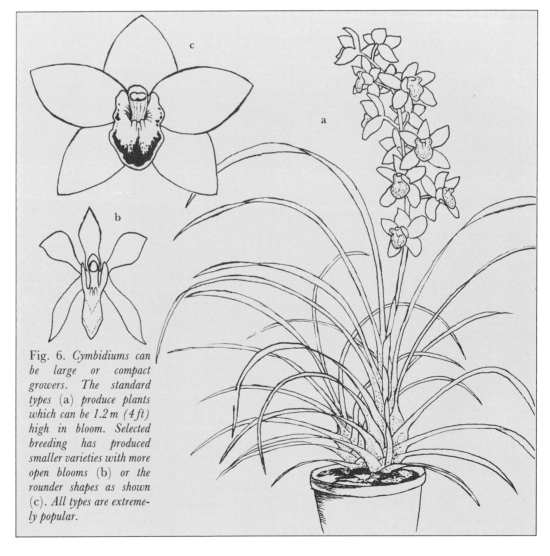

Fig. 6. *Cymbidiums can be large or compact growers. The standard types* (a) *produce plants which can be 1.2 m (4 ft) high in bloom. Selected breeding has produced smaller varieties with more open blooms* (b) *or the rounder shapes as shown* (c). *All types are extremely popular.*

Like so many of our orchids today the *Cymbidium* species have become scarce and should not be handled by the beginner. The hybrids are far more suitable for the home grower. As with all other orchids, new varieties are produced by crossing two selected parents. The seedlings produce a wider range of plants which will bear some resemblance to each parent, but, like children in a family, no two will be exactly alike. With the introduction of mass propagation by meristem culture, the finest varieties have now been made readily available at reasonable prices. It is quite possible for small home growers to have top quality, awarded plants among their collections.

Unlike odontoglossums and cattleyas, cymbidiums have no closely related genera with which they can be interbred. Therefore all the hybrids available are produced from within the *Cymbidium* genus alone.

Compact Hybrids

Today the miniature or compact cymbidiums are more widely grown than the standard varieties. These compact hybrids have been produced from a limited number of species which are small in stature and which will produce flowers from a plant in an easily accommodated pot. The first compact cymbidiums were produced some sixty to seventy years ago, but at the time created little interest. They were, in fact, in advance of their time and in the last twenty years their popularity has increased enormously. The earliest hybrids were produced by crossing the species *Cymbidium pumilum*. This delightful little plant produces flower spikes about 10–12 cm (4–5 in) long, carrying somewhat insignificant blooms. Although it is not recommended for the hobbyist as it can be difficult to grow and is now scarce in the wild, when crossed with standard cymbidiums, the result is an ideal, compact plant with flower spikes to match. One of the first *C. pumilum* hybrids to create much interest arose when *C. pumilum* was crossed with the standard *Cymbidium* species *C. lowianum*, giving some idea of what could be achieved. As a first generation primary the flowers were plentiful but star-shaped, with narrow petals and sepals. This hybrid is called *C*. Pumilow. Later, when *C. pumilum* was crossed with the large modern hybrids, far better results were achieved and well-rounded flowers were produced in an almost endless range of colours. Once second generation crossings began to appear, even more improvement was made. Today the best of these hybrids are represented by the famous line of Showgirls, which are available in a multitude of pastel colours, mainly pink and white.

The second most important miniature *Cymbidium* used in hybridizing is *C. devonianum*, This plant has virtually no pseudobulbs and produces wide, dark green foliage, and a pendant flower spike with numerous flowers. These are olive green in their colouring, the sepals and petals overlaid with dark red lining and the lip purple. This plant has given rise to many beautiful hybrids mostly of dark rich colouring such as *C*. Touchstone 'Mahogany' AM/RHS which is a deep brown red. Other well-known varieties are *C*. Goblin, which is green, and *C*. Bulbarrow which has similar colouring to the parent species but with solid coloured lips.

From these two species, *C. pumilum* and *C. devonianum*, have arisen two completely different hybrid lines. The *C. pumilum* hybrids are recognizable by their clear pastel shades and delicately spotted lips, while in complete contrast the hybrids from *C. devonianum* are richly coloured, in reds and greens. The solid crimson colouring of the lips in *devonianum* hybrids makes these miniatures quite unique among cymbidiums, for this feature is not found in the standards to the same extent. The beauty of the miniatures is that they can be contained in as little as a 15 cm (6 in) pot, they are easily handled and do not present the problems which occur with handling massive standard cymbidiums. However, if allowed to grow on for several years without being divided, they can make very large specimen plants. Otherwise they can be kept small by dividing and removing back bulbs. Of course, the larger the plant, the more spikes produced in a season, resulting in a far better show of flowers. The *C. pumilum* hybrids produce upright spikes, while those bred from *C. devonianum* retain the pendant form, and will give a beautifully cascading or arching spray. Alternatively, if preferred, they can be trained in an upright position where sufficient headroom is available – it is a matter of personal choice.

Standard Hybrids

In contrast to the miniatures, the standard *Cymbidium* has been produced from a handful of species of the most decorative type. Here the hybridizer had continually strived to produce larger and rounder flowers in a wide range of colours and varieties. The best of these produce long, many-flowered spikes over 1 m (3 ft) high and are the result of many generations of interbreeding which has continued for decades. The hybrids seen today bear no resemblance to the species from which they originated. If one has the room in which to grow these plants, preferably a sun lounge, then these highly decorative orchids will produce a beautiful display in the winter and early spring. At this time of the year, when there are few flowers to grace the room, they are most welcome.

Some of the most popular varieties are *C.* Balkis and related hybrids, which produce perfectly round flowers in colours ranging from pure white, through many shades of cream and yellow, the pastel pinks which contain Vieux Rose in their parentage and are well known for their spotted lips, to the dark pinks and rich reds. In contrast to these are the vibrant greens of Nicky, Fort George and Miretta, which steal the stage with their red or spotted lips. Another exciting colour is yellow, which ranges from pale primrose to the golden yellow of Cariga and the pre-Christmas Angelica. With the exception of blue and its near shades, any colour can be found, and the beginner or novice grower may do better asking for a plant by colour rather than quoting a particular name to the nurseryman. With new hybrids arriving on the market so fast, some names can quickly become outdated. For complete satisfaction it is better to ask the nurseryman for a 'green *Cymbidium* with a red lip' and leave the choice of variety to him.

Cymbidiums grow all the year round, merely slowing the rate of their growth during the winter in accordance with the shorter days and lower temperatures. With their extensive root system they can absorb large quantities of water and this should not be restricted during the spring and summer when their growth is at its maximum. The watering should be reduced slightly during winter to keep the plants just evenly moist without allowing them to dry out completely. In imitation of their natural habitat's conditions they will also benefit from regular overhead spraying throughout the summer with an application of liquid feed every ten days or so.

ENCYCLIA

Among the encyclias are a number of extremely attractive species. The following species were, until recently, known as epidendrums, under which name they can be found in older books on the subject.

Encyclia cochleata (Fig. 7a) comes from Mexico, Guatemala and Honduras. The pseudobulbs are curiously shaped, with a narrow base swelling out into a club shape which carries a pair of broad, light green leaves. The flowering spike appears from in between these leaves in the spring, and a green sheath protects its early development. The spike can be any length, depending upon the size and strength of the plant. A very young plant will produce a couple of flowers on a short spike, while a large specimen will produce up to a hundred flowers, on a flower spike which may be 1 m (3 ft) tall. These flowers will not all open at once, but will be produced over many months in a steady succession of blooms. It is not unusual for a large plant to continue to bloom for over a year, by which time the next pseudobulb has been completed and is flowering in turn, so the plant becomes perpetually blooming. The individual flowers are green and black and the narrow petals and sepals form

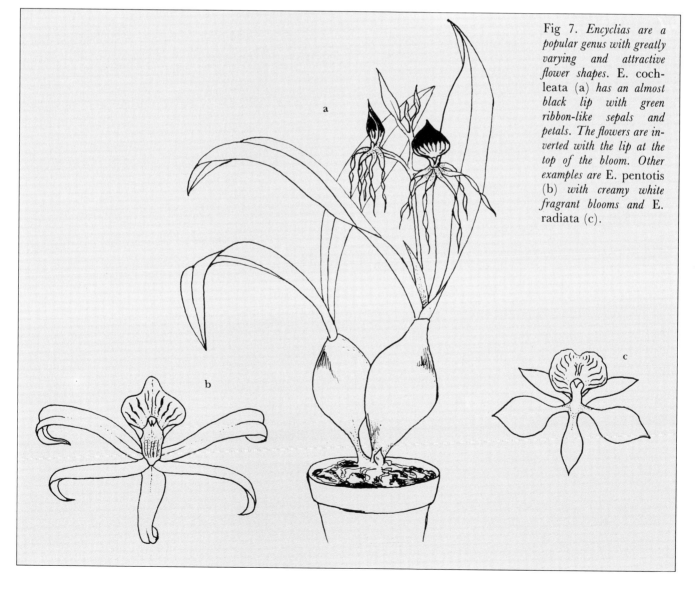

Fig 7. *Encyclias are a popular genus with greatly varying and attractive flower shapes. E. cochleata (a) has an almost black lip with green ribbon-like sepals and petals. The flowers are inverted with the lip at the top of the bloom. Other examples are* E. pentotis (b) *with creamy white fragrant blooms and* E. radiata (c).

twisted green ribbons. The rounded lip, which gives rise to this plant's common name of 'cockleshell orchid', is very dark, almost black in colour and is placed at the top of the flower. It is an unusual feature among orchids for the lip to be held uppermost on the flower.

Another example of an 'upside down flower' is *E. pentotis* (Fig. 7*b*). In this species the pseudobulbs are tall and slender and the two leaves are dark green. The two buds (ocasionally only one) emerge from the sheath and open on a very short stem which barely exceeds the length of the sheath. The two flowers open back to back, resembling alighting butterflies. The colouring of the petals and sepals is a light creamy green, and the lip is streaked with red. Although these flowers only last from two to three weeks in the early summer, they are accompanied by the most delightful fragrance. This variety is one of a whole group of similar species, including *E. radiata* (Fig. 7*c*) all of which have a pale off-white colouring with a red-lined lip, and are highly fragrant. Most require similar culture, and some may be tried along with *E. pentotis*.

A further interesting and showy species which does not resemble the above two, is *E. vitellina*. This also comes from Mexico and Guatemala. The pseudobulbs are small and the leaves a dark blue green with a delicate bloom, which is most apparent on the newly completed growths. The flower spikes, which carry many flowers, can be up to 30 cm (1 ft) tall, and on large plants they will branch once or twice. The star-shaped flowers are vermilion red, sometimes varying to orange red, and the small neat lip at the bottom of the flower is orange red. The main flowering season is spread through the summer and autumn months. Because there are very few red flowers among the orchids, this plant is especially desirable, and for brightness it is not easily surpassed. It likes to grow on the dry side, which makes it ideal for indoors, and it should always be kept in as small a pot as possible.

The encyclias are a very large and variable group of orchids; we have recommended only three species which, while hardly representative of the genus as a whole, do provide useful plants which may be added to a collection.

The encyclias recommended have a growing period followed by a resting period during which time they should be kept on the dry side, watering occasionally to prevent any shrivelling of the pseudobulbs. The plants can be given liquid feed during the most active months of the year when they should not be allowed to dry out. *E. vitellina* should be grown slightly drier than the other species at all times and the leaves should not be sprayed or wiped with water, which would remove the protective bloom.

ODONTOGLOSSUM *AND ALLIED HYBRIDS*

Odontoglossums come from the New World and nearly all are high altitude plants from the Andes. Although they grow close to the equator there, they enjoy the cool, airy conditions of the cloud forest high in the mountains, where there is little difference between the seasons and the days remain the same length all the year round. This produces an ideal climate of 'permanent spring' where the days are never too hot or the nights too cold. The modern hybrids produced in cultivation far from their natural habitat acclimatize easily to a temperate climate, provided they are given plenty of fresh air to keep them cool in the summer and artificial heat during the winter. Because these conditions are not easily met in the home, they are not very successful as houseplants. However,

Encyclia vitellina *A most charming species with the brightest colour of any in the genus. Flowering time can be variable, but mostly it blooms during the spring and early summer. Will grow on a cool, light window sill.*

when odontoglossums are crossed with closely related genera, hybrids are produced with a vigour which makes them far more suitable for indoor growing.

Not all the odontoglossums or their close relations originate from South America; there is a large branch of this family which comes from north of the Panama isthmus, including the region up through Guatemala to Mexico. Naturally, with such a wide distribution there is considerable variation in the habit of the plants and type of flowers they produce, although all require similar culture.

Odontoglossums are bulbous orchids, producing a new pseudobulb each growing season. A plant of flowering size may consist of four to five pseudobulbs with a new growth. As the young plant progresses to maturity, each pseudobulb produced is larger and more vigorous than the previous one, but this is only achieved with correct culture. Each pseudobulb may carry two to three leaves which will last for several years, the old pseudobulbs shedding their leaves first. An average plant consisting of five pseudobulbs will probably have two without leaf, the three younger pseudobulbs carrying between six and ten leaves between them. As the new growth reaches maturity and develops its pseudobulb, the flower spike will appear from the base. Depending upon the variety it may carry two or three or up to a dozen or more flowers, often on a tall arching spray. The flowering period is mainly during the spring or autumn months.

Before discussing the best plants to grow and the hybrids within this genus it is important to look at two other related genera with which odontoglossums will interbreed to produce much easier plants to grow.

The soft-leaved *Miltoniopsis*, (previously *Miltonia*) comes from the same Andean rain forest as the *Odontoglossum*, where it also grows upon the trees as an epiphyte (Fig. 8). Miltoniopsis have achieved a similar habit of growth although with smaller pseudobulbs and much more foliage, which is a beautiful soft green. Their flamboyant blooms are large and rounded and extremely colourful, and are often called 'pansy orchids' owing to the large round shape of the flower which resembles this popular bedding plant.

Oncidium is a much larger genus with a greater diversity of flower, colour, shape and size, and is widely distributed throughout the tropics of both North and South America. The habit of growth and structure of pseudobulbs more closely resemble the species among the odontoglossums.

Odontoglossum Species

There are still quite a number of *Odontoglossum* species which are obtainable and suitable for growing indoors. Although becoming scarce in the wild they propagate readily in the commercial greenhouses.

Odontoglossum species which may be tried as houseplants include *O. bictoniense* (Fig. 9), a soft, green-leaved species from Mexico which is continuously growing and which produces long upright sprays of up to twenty-five pretty flowers. The petals are green barred with brown, the heart-shaped lip is white often suffused with pink. Flowering during the summer, it will continue to bloom for many weeks. *O. pulchellum* has pure white flowers with yellow centres which are produced from oval pseudobulbs which bear two narrow leaves. This species is fragrant and also comes from Mexico. It propagates and divides easily. None of the South American species of *Odontoglossum* or *Miltoniopsis* is available these days as houseplants. They will only be found in cultivation in limited quantities in botanical collections where they have become collectors' items, or in the 'stud' houses of orchid breeders.

Oncidium Species

Among the *Oncidium* species which are readily available and recommended for indoor growing are *O. flexuosum*, which has a habit of growth closely resembling that of the odontoglossums with a long rhizome, while the flowers are carried at the top of long branched sprays. The most prominent feature of all oncidiums is the lip, and that of *O. flexuosum* is no exception. This is large and rounded, and coloured a

SOME ORCHIDS TO GROW

Fig. 8. *Miltoniopsis give large showy blooms on a neatly growing plant. They have brightly coloured gay flowers with some fragrance, mainly summer flowering. A fine range of hybrids is available.*

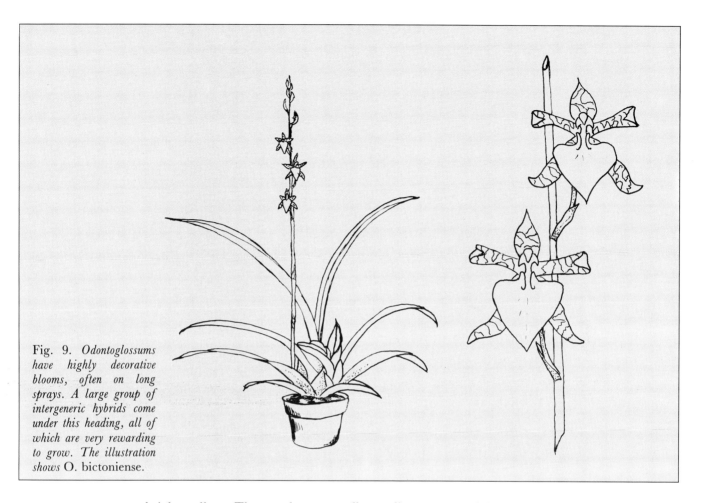

Fig. 9. *Odontoglossums have highly decorative blooms, often on long sprays. A large group of intergeneric hybrids come under this heading, all of which are very rewarding to grow. The illustration shows* O. bictoniense.

bright yellow. The petals are smaller, yellow patterned in brown. *O. ornithorynchum*, by contrast, produces short, branched sprays of numerous, densely clustered, rosy pink flowers with twisted and curled petals. This species is often grown solely for its beautiful fragrance. *O. incurvum* has long, branched spikes of pale pink flowers and white lips. Up to a hundred blooms are produced on a spray. *O. flexuosum, O. ornithorynchum* and *O. incurvum* all come from Mexico, where they are used to growing in a drier atmosphere than some of the jungle plants, making them more easily adaptable to culture indoors.

Multigeneric Hybrids

As already mentioned, the *Odontoglossum* species from South America are not to be recommended for indoors. However, the numerous hybrids from them are worth trying particularly where they have been crossed with *Miltoniopsis* to produce the genus *Odontonia*, or with *Oncidium* to produce *Odontocidium*. The little-known genus *Cochlioda*, which is seldom seen in cultivation today, produces bright red flowers and has been used extensively for breeding with *Odontoglossum* species to produce the genus *Odontioda*. When an *Odontioda* hybrid is crossed with a *Miltoniopsis* the result is a trigeneric cross. This was first achieved by a Belgian grower, Mr Vuylsteke, who gave his hybrid the new generic name of *Vuylstekeara*. Another example is the genus *Wilsonara*, which is the result of combining *Odontoglossum, Cochlioda* and *Oncidium*.

These complex hybrids are extremely difficult to breed, but once they

Opposite: Oncidium flexuosum. *A plant in need of good light, grown on the window sill to achieve flowering. A long slender flower spike produces many little branches at the top, on which are carried dozens of small, bright yellow flowers.*

Odontocidium *Tiger-butter. This attractive modern hybrid produces many flowers on a long spike from a plant smaller than the cymbidium. Plants in this group will bloom approximately every nine months.*

have been produced they are usually very easy to grow. Because of the different species represented in the one hybrid they are much stronger and more vigorous in cultivation and the flowers bear the best characteristics of shape and size from the different parents. One of the most famous hybrids available today is *Vuylstekeara* Cambria 'Plush' FCC/RHS (First Class Certificate awarded by The Royal Horticultural Society, London). This outstanding plant, which was originally raised in the 1930s, has never been superseded and with modern methods of mass propagation is available for everyone to grow. It produces long sprays of deep, wine red flowers, with a large spreading white lip heavily peppered with red. Today this plant has become popular all over the world, and because of its complicated breeding it will adapt to growing in warm or cool conditions.

Odontocidium Tigerbutter is a hybrid from *Oncidium tigrinum* in which the characteristics of that fine species have been enhanced to produce a rounded flower with a large yellow lip and broad glossy petals which far surpass the species flower.

Wilsonara Widecombe Fair is, by contrast, a very open, star-shaped bloom which is a first generation hybrid from *Oncidium incurvum*. A large plant will produce a hundred flowers on a massive branched spike.

These hybrids and many others are best grown in a cool room where the light is good but away from all direct sunshine. The same applies to the numerous and excellent *Miltoniopsis* hybrids which are so readily available today, and are obtainable in reds, whites, yellows and plum as well as pinks and endless combinations of these shades.

The multigeneric hybrids are continuously growing plants. The only time they are not growing is when they are producing their flower spikes. Because the new growth follows immediately after the plant has finished flowering, these plants should be kept watered throughout the year. They can be allowed to dry out slightly during the winter months, but otherwise the compost must be kept evenly moist to encourage a steady, continuous rate of growth. Among the species, those varieties which do not rest, such as *Odontoglossum bictoniense*, should be watered as the hybrids, while those which cease their growth during part or all of the winter should be allowed to dry out, although not to such an extent that their pseudobulbs shrivel. Should this occur, give one very thorough watering and keep the plants slightly wetter until the pseudo-bulbs regain their plumpness.

Odontonia *Mena. This colourful hybrid shows the typical patterning on the sepals and petals which makes this group quite distinct. Arching flower spikes will need some support.*

PAPHIOPEDILUM

These are the well-known and popular 'lady's slipper' orchids, so named because the lip has developed into a large pouch resembling a slipper. They were among the first orchids to be cultivated as house-plants and were a common sight in the Wardian cases of Victorian drawing rooms. In older books you will find them referred to as cypripediums. This large group of orchids was later divided, and the cypripediums of the modern classification are quite unsuitable as house-plants, as well as being difficult to obtain.

Paphiopedilum species are widely distributed throughout the Far East, stretching from China and Himalayas in the far north to the islands of the Philippines, all the way down to Malaysia and south to New

Opposite: Odontioda Harrods Forever. A group of these colourful hybrids can produce their flowers at different times throughout the year, although mostly they bloom in the spring months. Suitable for a window sill situation.

Above: Miltoniopsis Andy Easton. These delightful 'Pansy Orchids' produce large flowers from modest-sized plants. They are extremely compact and easy to grow. Will bloom twice a year, in the summer and again in the winter. Flowers fragrant.

Guinea. The species are usually terrestrial in habit, growing in the ground among other shade-loving vegetation. Occasionally some may be found growing as epiphytes on the lower branches of trees. Unlike most orchids, the plants do not have pseudobulbs but produce growths, each consisting of five or six leaves. (Fig. 10a). New growths are added each year and are joined together by an underground rhizome. The colour of the leaves may vary considerably, some being plain dark green while others have a red or mauve flecking at the base and on the undersides of the foliage. Other types are mottled all over in a contrasting light and dark pattern. It is these beautiful leaves which make these orchids particularly attractive as foliage plants all the year round.

Their flowers are extremely long-lasting, often remaining for eight to ten weeks in perfection, and this is one reason why they were among the first orchids to be hybridized. So successful has this been that today the hobbyist can choose from an enormous range of types and colours. Some typical varieties produce a single bloom on a long stem, while others of different descent will give three or four flowers on a spray. Further varieties will bloom in succession, producing a number of flowers over a period of twelve months, so remaining nearly always in bloom. Paphiopedilums are so popular as houseplants, particularly in Europe, that vast quantities are produced by nurserymen in an almost unlimited range of colours, shapes and sizes. The flowering period is mainly during the winter months, although with new varieties continually appearing on the market, it is possible, with careful selection, to have blooms all the year round.

Choosing a Paphiopedilum

For indoor growing, the beginner should start with mature, flowering-sized plants, and not be tempted to start immediately trying to divide and propagate the plants until considerable experience has been gained. The full beauty of these orchids often cannot be realized until they are specimen plants which have been allowed to grow on for several years without continual division. These specimen plants will produce several flowers each year from the new growths, providing months of bloom.

Generally, the green-leaved varieties require slightly cooler conditions than the heavily mottled varieties, although it is not impossible to grow them together with careful attention to the temperature. As shade-loving plants they should never be exposed to bright sunlight and should not be grown on a very sunny window sill unless they are fully protected from the fiercest sun in the summer months. Their delicate foliage can easily become scorched by sun through glass.

The paphiopedilums make ideal plants for an orchid case; their size is easily accommodated, and they will benefit from the fairly constant temperature between summer and winter, day and night. Because they are continuously growing and do not have a resting period they enjoy fairly warm, comfortable conditions all the year round. In the orchid case they will be fully protected from cold draughts and from bright sunlight.

Since they do not possess pseudobulbs, their only food reserve is held in the fleshy leaves and thick roots. Consequently, they should not be allowed to become dry at any time. The compost should be kept evenly moist, and it is important that the compost be open and very well drained to avoid saturation and damage to the root system. The plants

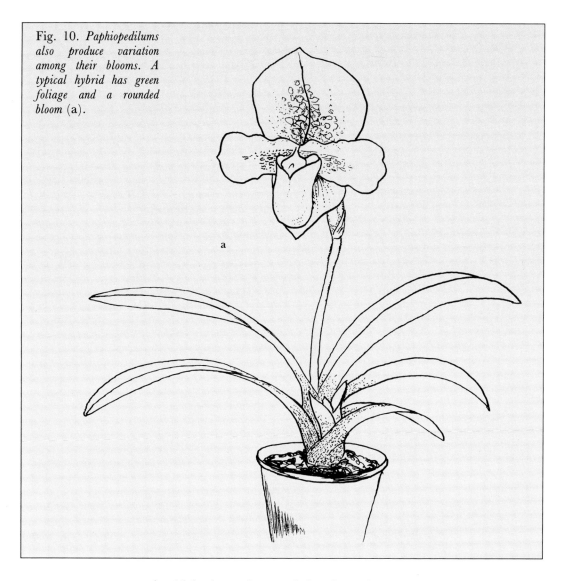

Fig. 10. *Paphiopedilums also produce variation among their blooms. A typical hybrid has green foliage and a rounded bloom* (a).

a

should be kept clean and free from dust by regular sponging of the leaves, although direct spraying is to be avoided. The plants like to be grown in as small a pot as possible, and repotted only when necessary, about every second or third year.

The modern hybrid will have several different species in its back-ground, bringing together the various qualities the species have to offer, and producing a plant quite unlike anything found in nature. All the species are extremely decorative plants, and were every bit as popular as the larger and more flamboyant hybrids until about a decade ago. Since that time most of these well-loved species are no longer available, owing to abuse in the form of over-collecting, and the spread of agriculture which destroys their native habitat. Another contributory factor is the new conservation laws which have recently come into force in an attempt to protect the species which remain in the wild. The loss of the species in cultivation has led to a greater demand for the hybrids, which in many cases are far better suited to cultivation indoors. With the combined qualities which have been bred into the hybrids the result is a stronger and more vigorous plant which has a built-in tolerance to artificial conditions. For this reason *Paphiopedilum* species are not recommended for the beginner to start with, but they are mentioned where they have had influence in the making of the hybrids. Also, very few hybrids have been mentioned by name. It must be remembered that thousands of hybrids exist and it would be misleading and pointless to give a list of names. Instead we have mentioned lines of breeding, and the species which have made them possible, to give the reader an insight to the types which are available. Paphiopedilums are the only orchids among the most popular varieties that cannot be raised by the mass propagation method known as meristemming. This means that all the plants which are available have been produced by seed or conventional propagation by division.

Hybrid Origins

Among the hybrids are the well-loved types which produce large, well-rounded flowers of a heavy texture. These come in a variety of colours from lime green and clear yellow to rich dark reds and bronzes with any number of shades in between, and carrying various spots and stripes. These are the types which, although many times removed from the species, can be traced back through their pedigree to *Paphiopedilum insigne* and its many varieties (including the yellow form *P. insigne* var. *sanderae*), and also *P. bellatulum*. It was the combination of these two completely different paphiopedilums which formed the base for the modern breeding lines.

P. insigne orginates from the Himalayas. It is a green-leaved species, with slender foliage. The flowers are carried singly on tall, slender stems and last for many weeks during the winter. The flowers are greeny bronze, the dorsal petal white, shading to green at the base and spotted with brownish purple. The variety *sanderae* is pure yellow throughout, which provided the hybridizers with a completely different colour line for breeding. The main contributions of this species to the early hybrids were colouring and length of stem.

P. bellatulum, which comes from Thailand, represents a different group within this genus, and produces small, neat growths with beautifully marbled foliage. The leaves are thick and brittle, easily snapped like a young carrot. The flowers are produced from an exceedingly short stem and 'sit' neatly on top of the diminutive foliage. These blooms, which are produced singly, are perfectly round in shape and coloured a soft powdery white with heavy, dark red spotting. When crossed with *P. insigne* it passed its rounded shapes to the hybrids.

Other species which have played a part in producing the range of colorations, shapes of flower and lengths of stem available amongst the *Paphiopedilum* hybrids, are *P. spicerianum*, *P. villosum* and *P. fairieanum*. From the smaller growing *P. niveum*, which comes from Thailand and Malaysia and produces dainty, well-rounded white flowers on a medium stem, have come a host of white and pastel hybrids with delicate spotting or flushing.

Opposite: Miltoniopsis Emotion 'Redbreast'. Colours in this genus are restricted to white, red, pink and light yellow, in an endless combination of shades. These plants do not need strong light and should be kept in a shady position.

The mottled-leaved paphiopedilums give a different type of flower, having been produced from a different range of species. These mottled types are noted for their lighter, more open flower. These are carried singly on a tall slender stem, the dorsal petal being large and vertically striped, while the narrower petals are generally more vertical, embracing the pouch. An important species in this group is *P. callosum* and its coloured forms. This lovely species from Thailand has everything to commend it. The graceful flowers are green and purple, and the dorsal

is white, flamed with purple. From this and several related species comes a further range of hybrids, where selective breeding has given rise to many different colours, including clear apple green through red and purple in rich hues. These mottled-leaved types are also extremely long lasting, and will bloom freely throughout the year (Fig. 10*b*).

A further group of paphiopedilums comes from the Philippines and has produced the unique varieties which give the multi-flowering stems with three to four flowers on a spray. These flowers are more slender in shape, with longer, narrower petals, and the dorsal petal is usually smaller than in the more conventional types. These hybrids are less in number and often do not go back through so many generations. This means that the resemblance to the original species is more noticeable and the colourings are more subtle, being represented by pink, beige and light green or brown (Fig. 10*c*). Two species which have helped to produce these unusual hybrids are *P. philippinense* and *P. haynaldianum*. *P. philippinense* produces several striking blooms, richly coloured in dark purple. The petals are long, narrow and often twisted along their length. They extend to well below the pouch. *P. haynaldianum* is lightly coloured in green and pink with several large flowers well spaced along a tall stem. The dorsal petal and pouch are small while the other petals are elongated, and adorned with spots toward the centre of the flower. *P. chamberlainianum* is a related species which comes from Malaysia and produces numerous blooms one at a time in a succession which will continue for twelve months or more. Recent breeding from this species and its various coloured forms is producing yet another range of alternative hybrids which have slightly smaller flowers, more compact in shape and showing green and pink or yellow in their colouring. These flowers are often adorned with short hairs along the crest of the petals, which are held horizontally to the small pouch and dorsal petal.

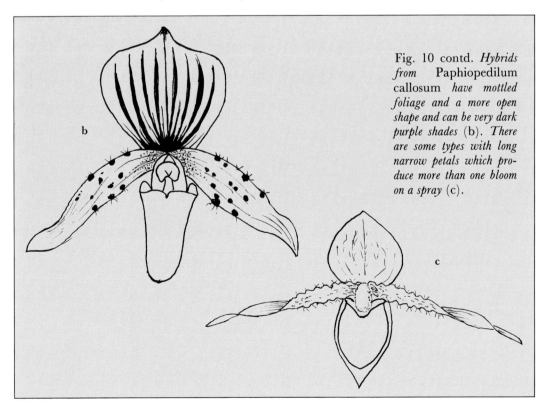

Fig. 10 contd. *Hybrids from* Paphiopedilum callosum *have mottled foliage and a more open shape and can be very dark purple shades* (b). *There are some types with long narrow petals which produce more than one bloom on a spray* (c).

PHALAENOPSIS

Phalaenopsis are extremely beautiful orchids, with species to be found in India, down through Malaysia and Borneo to New Guinea, with the largest concentrations in the Philippines. They grow mainly in the steamy lowland forests where there is a constant moist atmosphere and very little direct sunlight. The plants live upon host trees as epiphytes and often grown downwards.

Phalaenopsis do not produce pseudobulbs but their leaves are extremely thick and fleshy and grow from the base of the plant. Usually one or two new leaves are produced from the centre of the plant in a season (Fig. 11*a*). An average-sized plant in cultivation may have between three and six leaves at any one time and in some species they can grow to over 1 m (3 ft) in length. They may be plain dark green, or

Paphiopedilum. *The green or plain-leaved hybrids have very dramatic, round flowers. These plants like to be warm and shady. The large single blooms will last for eight weeks in the winter.*

beautifully mottled and barred in silvery grey. The roots of the phalaenopsis are the most attractive of any orchids; in the wild they attach themselves firmly to the bark of their tree, and run along its surface for some distance. These very fleshy roots are flat, silvery grey with a green or purple growing tip. In cultivation they will adhere to anything with which they come into contact. The flower spikes appear from the base of one of the younger leaves and can carry from just a few to many, well-rounded flat blooms.

Unlike so many orchids, the *Phalaenopsis* hybrids do not have a definite flowering season; owing to the various species in their make-up they tend to bloom at any time of the year and will last for many weeks in perfection. A large mature plant will often produce a new flower spike before the old one has finished flowering, with the result that a single plant can remain in bloom for many months. A further desirable feature of the phalaenopsis is that the flower spike, when it has finished blooming, will produce further side shoots which in turn will have more

Paphiopedilum Capa-blanca. This is a much older hybrid, with a more 'open' flower which is pre-ferred by some growers. These shade-loving orchids will bloom once a year during the winter.

flowers. The colours of the phalaenopsis, although restricted basically to pink and white with a little yellow, come in a variety of shades with different markings. It is not unusual for young plants also to be produced from the tip of the side shoots on an old flower spike, and it is these which are used in propagation. While many of the species do this quite freely on a regular basis, most of the hybrids are more reluctant to produce offspring in this way, although it does occasionally happen.

Recommended Species

Phalaenopsis are related to a number of different orchids, including vandas, renantheras and doritis with which they will interbreed to produce intergeneric hybrids. However, these crossings greatly alter the growing requirements of the hybrid, which can become more demanding in its requirements for light. Generally speaking, the home orchid grower will find the pure-bred phalaenopsis far more easily

Paphiopedilum Maudiae. The elegant green flower of a mottled-leaved hybrid which likes to be grown in a warm, shady place, either inside a growing case or on the window sill away from strong light. Blooms once or twice a year.

accommodated than the bigeneric hybrids, unless there is a very sunny position available. The pure-bred *Phalaenopsis* hybrids are also often more free-flowering.

Many of the *Phalaenopsis* species, especially those from the Malaysian Peninsula, are becoming scarce in cultivation as they dwindle in the wild. The species which are still common are mostly those from the Philippines, such as *P. amabilis*, *P. sanderana*, *P. stuartiana* and *P. schilleriana*. These delightful, free-flowering species have formed the basis for the majority of the modern hybrids. From *P. sanderiana* and *P. schilleriana* have come the pink varieties, while *P. amabilis* has produced all the large, modern white varieties and *P. stuartiana* has added the attractive spotting of the lower petals and a variety of delightful lip markings.

Other hybrid types are being created by crossing these modern round hybrids (Fig. 11*b*) with the smaller flowered species, such as *P. lueddemanniana* to give a further range of novelty types. These novelties often produce a much smaller plant with compact flowers (Fig. 11*c*).

Fig. 11. *Phalaenopsis make successful plants in a warm environment. Compact hybrids (a and b) are ideal for an indoor growing case, while the larger types (c) can produce flower spikes up to 1 m (3 ft) tall. These orchids will remain in bloom longer than any other type.*

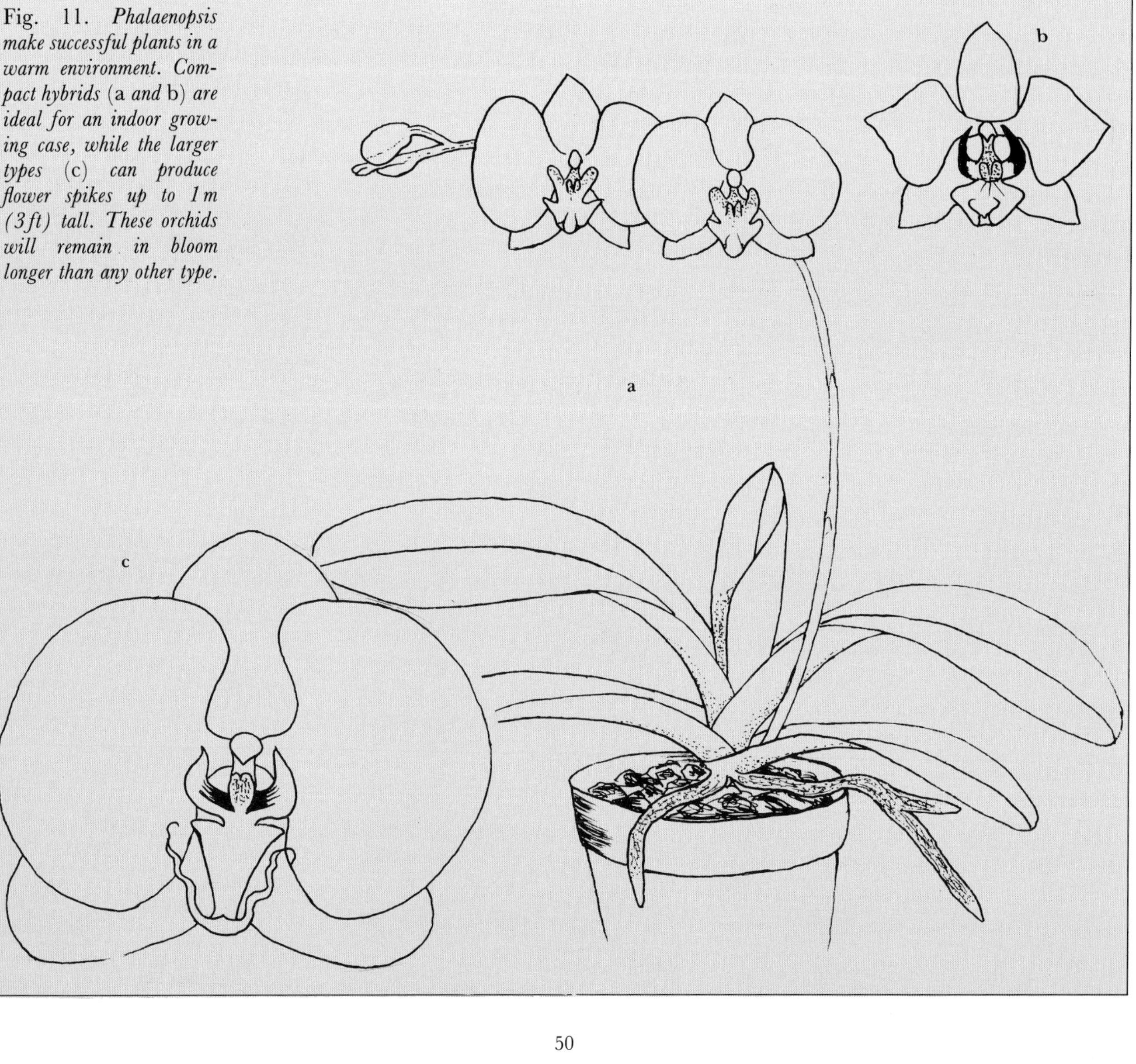

Phalaenopsis *Cashmore. A warm position with not too much light suits the lovely 'Moth Orchid'. An indoor growing case is ideal. Flowers can be expected at any time, two or three bloomings a year.*

Cultivation

Phalaenopsis are warm-growing orchids which cannot stand the cooler temperatures of many of their counterparts. They would not be very happy standing on the kitchen window sill or in a living room unless it remained very warm during the day and night. Ideally their minimum night temperature should never drop below 18°C (65°F) and they are even happier with a minimum of 21°C (70°F). The ideal place for growing phalaenopsis is an indoor growing case, where the temperature can be controlled and kept up to their minimum requirements. They also make very good subjects for the growing case because they do not require very much light to grow and flower well, and the artificial light suits them well. A number of the hybrids produce very long flower spikes when they are mature, and this should be borne in mind when placing them in the case. Their aerial roots will quickly adhere to the back or sides of the case, and this makes it difficult to move them once they have been positioned, without causing unnecessary damage. Another advantage of growing phalaenopsis in the confines of a case is that the humidity can be kept that bit higher than for the other orchids growing in the room.

The compost in which phalaenopsis are grown should always be kept moist; the plants must not be allowed to become overwet at any time, nor completely dry for any period. More often than not their long fleshy roots will extend over the rim of the pot to seek moisture wherever they can find it, which may include the bottom of the water-filled humidity tray. These roots should be allowed to meander and are often healthier than those made inside the pot. The plants can be given additional liquid feed throughout the year when artificial daylight is available to them. Spraying should be done in moderation only – too much water on the surface of the leaves can cause spotting and, at worst, rotting at the centre of the plant.

For anyone who is considering growing phalaenopsis for the first time, the hybrids would be the obvious choice. As so often happens with breeding, the best qualities of the species are carried forward and

Phalaenopsis *Lipperot. Colours in this group are restricted to pink and white, also yellow. Wonderfully free-flowering orchids, they are among the most rewarding for the indoor grower.*

Dendrobium nobile. *This species, and the many colourful hybrids raised from it, all like plenty of light in which to bloom. If not enough light is available indoors they can be grown out-of-doors for the summer.*

combined in the hybrid to produce a much more robust plant which is more resistant to neglect. There is a much wider choice of colour and size among the hybrids, and plants can be chosen to fit into the amount of space available, bearing in mind the amount of head room which can be given to the plants. Where a number of phalaenopsis plants are grown together, it is possible to have blooms all the year round, although one would need at least a dozen plants to achieve this perpetual display.

Phalaenopsis are also in great demand in many parts of the world for their cut flowers, which are held in high regard by florists. In Europe especially, they are extensively cultivated for this market. Usually pure white varieties are grown, which are then dyed whichever colour is required in the same way that carnations are dyed. Phalaenopsis would be grown even more extensively by the amateur orchid grower if it were not for the fact that their high temperature requirements make them very expensive to cultivate in greenhouses. The home grower can grow them much more cheaply in an indoor case.

FURTHER GENERA AND VARIETIES

DENDROBIUM

This is a large genus of which a comparatively few are grown indoors. *D. nobile* types (Fig. 12*a*) like much light all the year round, which is not always possible to give. Most rewarding indoors are a few of the Indian species such as *D. infundibulum* (Fig. 12*b*), which has large heads of white blooms approximately 8 cm (3 in) across. These come in the early spring from the top of evergreen canes 30 cm (12 in) tall. These orchids need to be grown cool and rested in the winter.

EPIDENDRUM

Dendrobium infundibulum. *A delightful species which produces 'canes' with heads of flowers from the top of the previous years' canes. These will last for several weeks in the spring. Grows in good light and rests in the winter.*

There are not many epidendrum species suitable for indoors because of their size, but where a roomy sun lounge or lean-to conservatory wants something large to brighten it up, then *E. ibaguense* (syn. *E. radicans*) a species from Mexico, would be perfect. This plant produces tall, reed-like stems with dark leaves and blooms from the top of a long stem. Large heads of bright red flowers are produced all the year round. A mature plant can reach 2 m (6 ft) tall and be perpetually in bloom. Water all the year round. It will grow cool or intermediate.

54

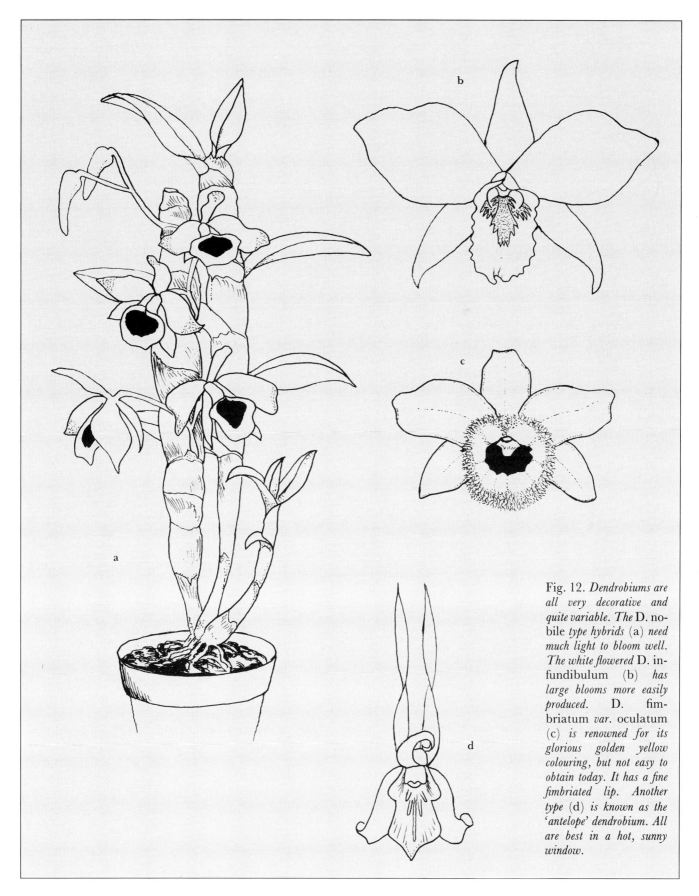

Fig. 12. *Dendrobiums are all very decorative and quite variable. The* D. nobile *type hybrids* (a) *need much light to bloom well. The white flowered* D. infundibulum (b) *has large blooms more easily produced.* D. fimbriatum *var.* oculatum (c) *is renowned for its glorious golden yellow colouring, but not easy to obtain today. It has a fine fimbriated lip. Another type* (d) *is known as the 'antelope' dendrobium. All are best in a hot, sunny window.*

LYCASTE

These are mostly large plants, with pseudobulbs which become decid-uous in winter when the plant is resting. The distinctive, three-cornered, single blooms are most attractive, usually coming in the spring from the base of the pseudobulb at the start of the growing season. Both species and hybrids can be grown in a light position where there is room for their large spreading leaves in the summer. All originate from South and Central America. *L*. Auburn is a lovely hybrid to grow which varies in its colour from creamy white to pink,.

MASDEVALLIA

These South American orchids are sometimes referred to as 'kite' orchids, the name reflecting the flower shape which often has long 'tails', and the fact that the solitary blooms can come on tall slender stems well above the foliage (Fig. 13). Not all are like this, however – in some varieties the blooms nestle among the foliage. They are evergreen and do not make pseudobulbs. Their flowering time is mainly summer. Grow cool and keep moist all year round. Both hybrids and species are grown. *M. kimballiana* combines many qualities of this brightly coloured genus.

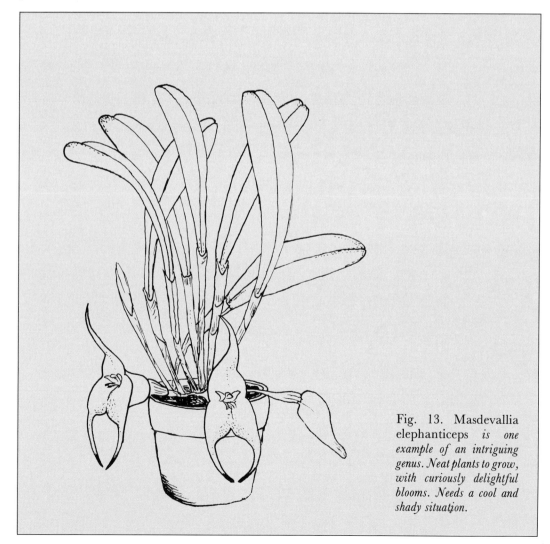

Fig. 13. Masdevallia elephanticeps *is one example of an intriguing genus. Neat plants to grow, with curiously delightful blooms. Needs a cool and shady situation.*

MAXILLARIA

These are mostly small plants with pseudobulbs easily accommodated in a limited space. Flowering times are spring and summer. Mostly South American species are grown, which should be kept cool and allowed to rest in the winter. *M. picta* is yellow, winter flowering and fragrant. *M. ochroluca* produces numerous white blooms with yellow to orange centres and is fragrant. *M. praestans* has smart-looking tan-striped flowers throughout the summer.

PLEIONE

These delightful miniature orchids need to be grown very cool, and do best when kept during the winter at a temperature just above freezing. They are therefore one of a few types for a unheated conservatory, or unheated spare room. The pseudobulbs are small, deciduous and live for two years, always being replaced by the newer pseudobulbs. A dry rest is required in winter. *P. Alishan* is a most attractive hybrid from species originating from China and Formosa. It blooms early in the spring.

Lycaste *Auburn*. Deciduous orchids which bloom in the early summer before the foliage is complete. Many single-flowered stems can be produced from one pseudobulb, giving a grand display.

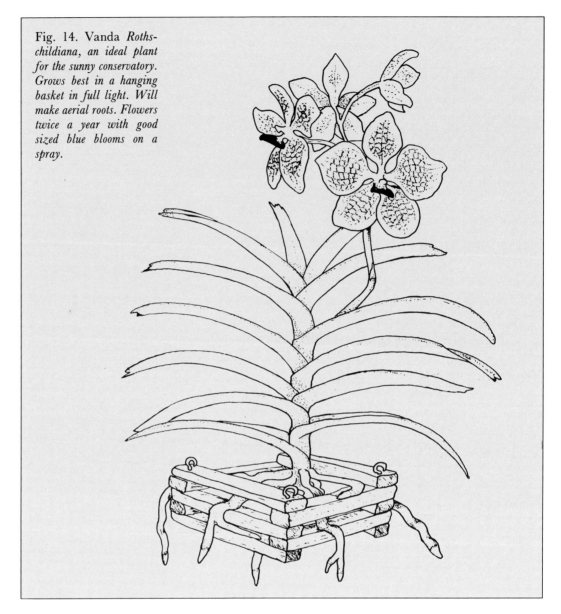

Fig. 14. Vanda *Roths-childiana, an ideal plant for the sunny conservatory. Grows best in a hanging basket in full light. Will make aerial roots. Flowers twice a year with good sized blue blooms on a spray.*

VANDA

Vandas can grow quite tall, up to 50 cm (18 in) or more with an upright, monopodial habit. They are 'high light' plants needing much light all year round to flower well. They grow best in open baskets suspended in a light position. (Fig. 14). They need a conservatory-type home and should be sprayed every day. Healthy plants can bloom up to three times a year. Species originate from India and Burma. Hybrids are more suitable for indoor growing. *V.* Rothschildiana is an exceptional dark blue hybrid which is easily the best variety to grow.

ZYGOPETALUM

These dramatic plants produce pseudobulbs and are quite large, making them most suitable for a broad window sill. Mostly hybrids are grown such as *Z.* Artur Elle which blooms during the winter with sprays of brown and violet blue fragrant blooms. They like to grow cool and moist all year round.

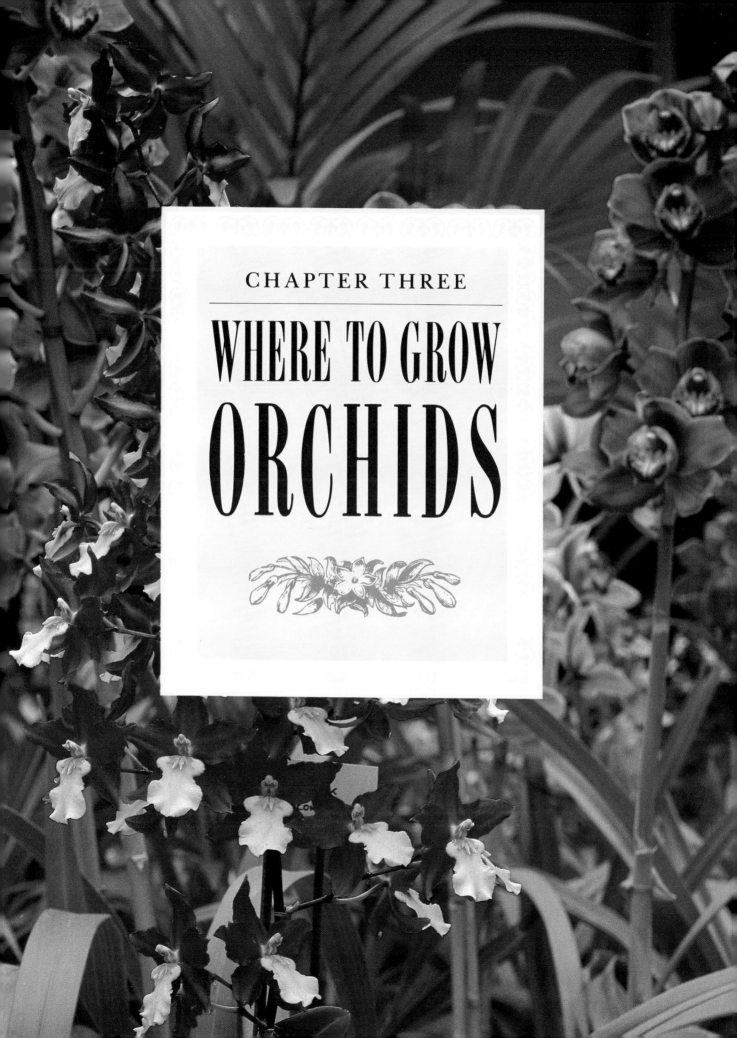

CHAPTER THREE

WHERE TO GROW
ORCHIDS

ADVANTAGES OF GROWING IN THE HOME

*G*rowing orchids in a greenhouse means that much time has to be spent creating the right conditions. An uncontrolled greenhouse can be an extremely dangerous place for its inhabitants. Left to its own devices, temperatures within will soar to 40°C plus (100°F plus) on a hot day and plunge to below freezing on winter nights. Not very hospitable for tropical plants coming from mountainous regions and used to cool, moist and the shady conditions!

The art of growing orchids in a greenhouse involves creating a totally artificial environment to suit the orchids, which then has to be maintained throughout the year. Only when this is mastered can strong and healthy plants be expected to grow. A good deal is added to the cost of keeping the plants, apart from the initial price of the greenhouse, in the form of heating equipment and shading materials which are the very basic requirements, fans for circulating the air, and possibly spraying and misting equipment. All of this can come to a considerable sum even before you have bought your first orchid.

Masdevallia Kimballiana. An example of the enchanting 'Kite Orchid'. A single flower is produced at the end of a slender stem. Its unusual shape and 'tail' makes it quite distinct. Flowers come twice a year in the summer and again in the winter.

Although there can be no doubt that a well-controlled and maintained greenhouse, in which the requirements of the orchids are paramount, will produce the finest of plants, the purpose of this book is to look into alternative methods of growing them, which do not require the same initial outlay to get started. If you have a sun lounge or conservatory, conditions in it are, to a lesser extent, also created to suit the orchids, but when we grow our plants indoors, the reverse is true, and the orchids are expected to cope with the conditions already found in the house. When only slight alterations can be made, it is surprising how easy it becomes to create a perfectly acceptable home for orchids which, when grown indoors, are not all that different from other houseplants, and in some cases are easier to cope with.

Other advantages of growing orchids indoors are that your plants are always close at hand and you will probably spend much more time in close proximity with them than you would in a greenhouse. This is particularly true of the housewife who spends more time at home. You quickly become more familiar with your plants, noting any changes in their growth, their watering requirements and so on. There is also the health and safety factor of the orchids to be considered. While a greenhouse left unattended for a day in adverse weather can be sufficient to cause lasting damage to the inhabitants, plants indoors are perfectly safe from extremes of temperature or rapid drying out. The far more gentle environment of the home will take much of the worry out of growing, and the need to be constantly in attendance.

There are, of course, areas in any room to avoid: the dark corners where little light reaches, places close to a source of heat such as an open fire, or on the mantelpiece above it. (This is often seen in advertisements for fireplaces, but is not much good for the plants!) The television set also gives off some heat, and this flow of warm dry air can be very dehydrating for orchids. The top of a tropical fish tank, however, could have the advantage of warm moist air rising from it, and provided there is sufficient light, a few orchids in bloom can complement the tropical fish and add considerably to the feature in the room. Where radiators are installed, plants should not be placed too close to them – again orchids will dehydrate rapidly if exposed to a stream of warm air. Keep them at least 60 cm (2 ft) away.

Before deciding upon a specific area in which to install your indoor orchids, there are three vital factors to be considered; temperature, light and shade.

TEMPERATURE

The majority of orchids suitable for indoor growing are referred to as 'cool'. The cool-growing types include cymbidiums, odontoglossums, dendrobiums, coelogynes, encyclias, maxillarias, masdevallias, some paphiopedilums, zygopetalums and many others. These orchids require a minimum night temperature of 10°C (50°F) in the winter, rising to 13°C (55°F) during the summer. A drop to 7°C (45°F) for a few hours occasionally during the winter will do little harm, but such a drop occuring every night for several months or weeks will, over a season, have a detrimental effect on growth. By the spring they may have wintered badly as a result and will take longer to commence growing again. Daytime temperatures will vary according to the time of year and the heating available in the home. During the winter it should rise by at least 6°C (10°F) to give a variation between day and night.

Summer daytime temperatures can rise safely to 30°C (86°F) maximum. While indoors these temperatures should not present a problem, (bearing in mind that anywhere between these limits will be suitable), in a conservatory or sun lounge the temperature could rise higher and it may be necessary to use blinds for shading.

Cattleyas, laelias, some oncidiums and paphiopedilums are among the most popular of the 'intermediate' orchids, requiring to be about 3°C (5°F) warmer at night. It is usually possible to find a room or certain position where the temperature is this bit warmer overnight.

The 'warm'-growing orchids are mainly the phalaenopsis, and for them and a few others an indoor growing case is probably most suitable, where a minimum night temperature of 16–19°C (61°–65°F) can be kept. Phalaenopsis will grow at lower temperatures, but will not succeed as well as when they are given this extra warmth. During the day this temperature can rise by 12°C (20°F). There should be little variation of these temperatures between summer and winter.

Lastly, the pleiones are different from the above groups, being semi-hardy. Ideally, they need only to be kept in a frost-free area for the winter, with cool culture during the summer growing season.

These recommended temperatures are meant as a guide, indicating the minimum and maximum ideal temperature required by the plants. As stated earlier, the orchids have come to live with you, and will be happy in a comfortable temperature range. A constant temperature, with little or no fluctuation between night and day is to be avoided. Too high a temperature, especially at night, is a common cause of orchids not flowering – a point to bear in mind.

Some cool orchids will grow happily alongside intermediate ones, where the temperature lies part way between their ideal requirements. Likewise, some intermediate types will grow with the warm ones; it is simply a case of trying them out in various positions. Temperature is only one aspect of successful growing.

In a conservatory, more attention should be paid to the temperature. With the greater area of glass it will behave like a greenhouse, making shading a necessity in summer, and some form of heating for the winter.

LIGHT

Most orchids, certainly those recommended for cool and intermediate growing, like plenty of light but not direct sunlight. They evolved growing on tree branches, high above the dense forest floor, but shaded by the foliage of the trees and exposed only to dapple sunlight overhead.

Indoors the light is obviously not as great as in a greenhouse or a conservatory. Even in a well-lit room the light will only come in from one direction, and this limited light has to be made full use of, unless artificial lights are to be installed. Generally, it is a case of giving the orchids every bit of light possible; it is almost impossible to give them too much light, while keeping them out of strong sun in summer.

Light is one factor in the home which you cannot increase – you can lessen the light but, without major alterations, you cannot increase it. Therefore, it is better to grow plants which will suit the light you have available. The light will vary from room to room according to its aspect. Most light will be obtained from a south-facing window and the least from a north-facing one. The size and nature of the windows will also determine how much light is available. Large picture windows in a modern house will let in far more light than small latticed windows in

Opposite: Pleione Ali-shan. These dainty little plants will grow any-where that is cool enough for them. A frost-free area is all that is required to have these delightful early spring flowers. Each bloom lasts about ten days. A large pan of pseudo-bulbs increases the flower-ing period.

an old cottage. Thick walls also limit the spread of the light. The ideal situation would be a south-facing window, offering enough light to cater even for those orchids requiring a lot of it (but see Shade, below). On the other hand, the place where orchids are most unlikely to succeed may be the bathroom. Although often warm and humid, it is usually the most ill-lit room in the house.

As with temperature, orchids can be divided into three main groups regarding the light requirement: 'high', 'medium' and 'low' light plants. The amount of light they require is in direct relation to their natural habitat in the wild, where their foliage and pseudobulbs have evolved to withstand a specific amount of light.

Cymbidiums, cattleyas and related hybrids, brassavolas, coelogynes, dendrobiums and vandas are all examples of high light orchids. These plants are best suited to the conservatory, sun lounge or large, well-lit bay window. Cymbidiums and cattleyas need space to grow in, and will not look their best in a confined area.

Maxillaria praestans. *A delightful miniature orchid suitable for the smallest window sill area. Plants as small as three pseudobulbs will bloom. Can also be grown on to a specimen for maximum effect.*

Medium light plants include odontoglossums and their related hybrids, lycastes, encyclias, zygopetalums, maxillarias and miltoniopsis. Most window sills would be suitable for them. They could also be grown among the high light plants but positioned so that they are partially shaded by them.

The low light plants are the paphiopedilums, masdevallias and phalaenopsis, among others. They would certainly suffer if given too much light, the foliage would turn yellow or whitish, and the phalaenopsis may become limp and dehydrated. These orchids are best suited to an area of limited light, but not dim, or an indoor growing case where the light can be regulated and controlled.

Orchids which have been grown with insufficient light will display dark green foliage which can become limp and floppy. Leaves may become extra long and narrow while the new growths will be weak and require some support.

SHADE

Shading the orchids indoors will not be necessary provided they are correctly positioned so as not to have the midday sun directly upon them. Morning or late afternoon sun passing over them for an hour or so will do nothing but good to the high and medium light plants. For plants in growing areas with artificial light, or set back from the window, the need for extra shade does not apply. In a conservatory, sun lounge or large bay window it may be necessary to give some protection from the direct sun and to reduce the temperature. Indoors, this can be easily achieved with net curtains or venetian blinds. Sun blinds on the outside of a conservatory will provide shade on the side, and if the roof is also glass, this can be given a coat of paint shading on the outside to cool the glass and reduce the sun's glare. Alternatively, if the roof does not get a lot of direct sun, nylon mesh, either inside or out will provide sufficient shade. It will depend upon the construction of the conservatory how easy this will be to fit.

Shading can also be of the natural kind, and a well-trained climber in the roof will give good shade to the orchids in the summer. However, this natural shading is not always totally satisfactory: an evergreen climber will not let sufficient light in during the winter and, as the climber rapidly grows, the shade becomes heavier each year, and it is not always noticed just how dark it is making the inside of the conservatory. Many climbing plants also become reluctant hosts to a number of pests, such as red spider mite or one of the many scale insects. These pests can then drop off on to the orchids below. This also applies to dead leaves and flowers. By all means grow your climbers, but do not expect your orchids to live permanently in their shadow!

SUITABLE HOMES FOR ORCHIDS

WINDOW SILL

Indoors, the most obvious place to put a few orchids is on the window sill. This will suit the high to medium light orchids (the low light types can be just as easily accommodated away from the window but still in an area of good light).

The only equipment needed to start off a small window sill collection of orchids is a humidity tray of the right size. These are available from garden centres in a range of attractive designs, usually made of plastic and in various shapes and sizes. The base of the tray can be covered with small pebbles, gravel, peat or similar material, to a depth of about 2.5 cm (1 in). Water is then poured in, to come about half way up the pebbles. This will allow the plants to stand on a dry base (they would not like to be standing in water), while a small amount of water evaporates around them to provide them with their own micro-climate of moist air. When placed in the tray the base of the plant should be level with the rim of the tray, so it may be necessary to stand the plant on an upturned saucer or flower pot to achieve the right height. If too low in the tray, the plant will not properly be seen or get enough light. Once a few plants are arranged in the tray, some greenery such as small attractive ferns can be placed in between or around the sides with their leaves fanning out around the tray but without covering up the orchids. In this position it should be possible to water the orchids without taking them out of the tray each time. Too much handling causes disturbance to the plants, as well as inadvertent damage to flower spikes etc. Should the water rise above the bottom of the orchid pots, it can be bailed out, which is easier to do if small stones have been used in the base. If peat has been used it should be replaced with new whenever it looks green and soured on the top. Pebbles will keep the water cleaner, and will only need to be washed and put back occasionally. Otherwise, there is very little maintainance required to keep your humidity tray of orchids looking good.

Those orchids most suited to window sill culture can be from the medium to high light range. Both types can be grown, keeping each in separate trays and positioned differently to take advantage of the light. Check also that those plants you have placed together require the same temperature range. Many orchids of this sort will be growing in pots under 15 cm (6 in) in diameter, so space need not be a problem.

Of course, a single plant can be grown on its own, and similar provision can be made for it to stand in a container with moisture at the base. It can also have its attending foliage plants to create a more pleasing and natural-looking effect. A single orchid would not object to sharing a tray with African violets, for example. These two vastly different plants are surprisingly compatible, and the essence of indoor growing should be the attractiveness of the exhibit. After all, in the home the plants are on permanent display for all to see and admire.

INDOOR GROWING CASE

There are several advantages to growing orchids by this method. First, as mentioned above, the orchids should provide an attractive permanent display, and this is superbly achieved in a case. Secondly, because the case will be totally artificially controlled, with the plants growing in unnatural light, it can be placed anywhere where the plants will be shown off to best effect and need not be restricted to the window areas. An otherwise dim corner of the room can be brought to life with a replica in miniature of a tropical rain forest. The plants can be placed permanently in position and will not need to be moved or taken out for watering, etc.

A simple case can be adapted from an aquarium or a glass room divider, or it can be a custom-built or home-made case which is in itself a beautiful piece of furniture. The custom-built case will come complete with finished backing with pockets in which to insert your plants, a

waterproofed gravel base where other small plants such as *Selaginella* can thrive, and controlled ventilation, temperature and light.

To grow orchids this way is simply a case of setting the thermostat to the correct levels as advised by the manufacturer and arranging your plants as you want them. Daily opening of the glass door for extra air during the summer, and regular watering, feeding and daily spraying are all that is required to maintain your miniature rain forest. The plants can either be growing in their pots, which in turn are placed in the 'pockets', or they may be removed from their pots and potted direct into the pockets. Some orchids could be tied on to a tree branch and this placed in the case. Ferns and other greenery can be added to enhance the overall effect. Some orchids will stand, in their pots, on the bottom of the case, which will be kept topped up with water from the watering of the plants above.

An old fish tank has found new occupants. With a moist base a number of small orchids can be grown here. Phalaenopsis may suit best, preferably with a growing light tube above.

Purpose-built cases as described here are not always easy to obtain, and most growers prefer to make their own, which can certainly be easier on the pocket. As with any enclosed area, the smaller it is, the less air there is within, and when contemplating making a case, it should be as large as possible, so as not to restrict too much the size of the orchids to be grown in it. The minimum measurements to be considered may be 60 × 90 cm and at least 90 cm high. (2 × 3 × 3 ft high). Apart from having front doors which will open to allow easy access to the plants and plenty of air, an opening in the top will allow a *flow* of air from the bottom to the top of the case.

The case can be built of wood, aluminium or tubular plastic framework, with obviously as much glass or perspex as possible. It may have a back to it or be designed to be seen from all angles. Depending upon the eventual size and the orchids to be grown in it, it may have one, two or more shelves, each one with a tray for retaining the water.

Coming right down in size, small terraria and ornamental cases are available for the growing of small plants, as well as the round 'goldfish bowl' glass bottles popularly sold for 'bottle gardens'. Such containers are too restricted for orchids to grow in, even for the very miniature varieties. The growing area is too confined to have any control over it, and the lack of air in a bottle would be a problem.

Artificial light is recommended for indoor cases to enable plants to be grown away from the window. A case standing in a window area to take advantage of the light would very quickly become overheated on a warm day. Window sill plants are better not contained within a case, but grown as described above. No artificial light has been devised which is as good as natural sunlight. Nevertheless, many orchids can be grown successfully under fluorescent lights designed for horticultural use, and these are available under various trade names from most garden centres or hardware shops. They are available in various sizes to fit most cases, and should be placed at least 15 cm (6 in) from the tallest leaves of the plants. There should then be no danger of the lights burning the leaves. For most orchids suited to this culture, 40 watt tubes are sufficient. The light intensity of the tubes will be greatest at the centre, and some slight differences can be taken advantage of by placing those plants in need of most light below the centre of the tube.

The greatest advantage of growing with artificial lights is that the 'daylight' hours can be controlled, and plants can benefit greatly during the winter months, when they can be given the same daylight hours as in the summer, up to 16 hours a day. This longer day length all the year round will compensate the plants for the lower intensity of light.

Those orchids best suited to this artificial environment are those warm-growing, low light plants which have little or no resting period, and can be relied upon to bloom throughout the year. Topping the list for suitability under these conditions are phalaenopsis and paphiopedilums; other plants which may be tried alongside them are miltoniopsis. The basic requirements are that the plants should be small or compact in growth, ideally have showy flowers during the winter, and grow and flower well under these conditions.

If the temperature and light factors within the case are too constant, this may well affect the blooming of the orchids. It will become necessary to vary the temperatures by at least 6°C (10°F) night and day, and also to vary the 'day length', from twelve hours in the winter, gradually increasing to sixteen hours maximum in the summer.

Opposite: *The ultimate in indoor growing is a specially designed orchid case. Equipped with lights, thermostat and humidity tray, once set up it will require very little maintenance while providing the orchids with their own microclimate.*

CELLAR CULTURE

In extremely cold countries where greenhouses are not practical because of the very severe winters, many growers successfully turn their cellars into growing rooms for orchids. This is a popular practice in parts of Canada and other countries where the hours of daylight during their long winters are too short to sustain the growth of orchids. Cellar culture in Britain (where only older houses were built with cellars) has yet to become popular but the method is described here briefly to show what is possible. If you are not lucky enough to have a cellar, there is no reason why an unused spare room should not be adapted in a similar way.

Cellars have the advantage of being well-insulated from outside weather conditions. Adapting them to grow orchids need not entail a considerable outlay and, unlike a greenhouse which is continually losing heat, the running costs are very low as there is virtually no heat loss.

Vanda Rothschildiana. The most rewarding of all the Vanda hybrids. Must be grown in good light and humidity. Will bloom two or three times a year. One of the finest blue orchids.

The orchids will be grown totally by artificial light. To this end the growing area within the cellar can be made to reflect as much of this as possible. The walls and ceiling can be painted white or lined with sheets of tin foil. The orchids will grow under the special light tubes designed for horticultural use. They can be installed on a time clock to work for twelve hours on, twelve hours off. By turning night into day and day into night, off-peak electricity can be used in the UK and thus savings can be made on running costs. An override switch can be installed to be switched on whenever you are attending to the plants.

Benches can be set up in the room in a similar way to a greenhouse, with provision being made to collect the surplus water from spraying and watering. To do this, place trays lined with expanded clay pellets or similar on the benches. Excess water will then collect in the trays and the floor will be kept dry (particularly important if this is a converted upstairs room). By standing the orchids on upturned pots above the wet base sufficient humidity should be created for them as the water should evaporate before the plants are watered again.

The lights, 40 watt fluorescent tubes, will need to cover the bench areas. Set them up in batches with white reflectors above them, and suspend them from the ceiling with a pulley system which will allow the lights to be raised or lowered. With complete insulation and some warmth generated from the light, very little other heating will be necessary. If it is, a small electric fan heater which moves the air around will be best. This can be thermostatically controlled to blow warm or cool air as necessary. Alternatively, where central heating is available it may be more practical to plumb in a small radiator off the system. If there is a window, this should be used to ventilate the basement or cellar at every opportunity, likewise an inside door left ajar may provide some air to keep it fresh over the plants.

Just as no two greenhouses are alike, so a cellar will behave in its own way. A grower setting up such an area will have to work out for himself how best to make it successful, with some trials in temperature fluctuation and light output even before any orchids are placed in it.

The watering and feeding of the plants will follow the same patttern as growing elsewhere.

By using a greater battery of lights on one side it will be possible to grow a wider range of orchids from the low and medium light ranges, and by varying the headroom above each bench plants of different heights can be accommodated.

When the orchids are finally placed in their new home, unless they have been growing elsewhere under artificial lighting, they should be given time to adjust to the new environment. Differences in the growth will become apparent after a few months. The size and shape of pseudobulbs will be seen to vary from earlier ones and the length of leaves may also be different. Colour changes in the foliage may also be noted as the plants respond directly to their new life style. Within twelve months they should become fully adjusted, the proof will be in their continued flowering and well-being.

Growing orchids under artificial lights may not be your first choice and is no substitute for real sunlight. Also, there is a limit to what will grow under these conditions, but for some it may prove to be the only way and is better than nothing. Orchids wintering in a cellar may be taken out of doors for their summer growing season to benefit from natural light for a few months of the year.

CONSERVATORIES

These are more popular than ever, with manufacturers offering a wide range of ingenious designs to suit all requirements. A conservatory can become a beautiful indoor garden, a place to grow those plants which will not survive out of doors, and what better plants than orchids! Most conservatories are roomy enough to house the larger of the cultivated types, such as cymbidiums, cattleyas and dendrobiums. With glass on all sides but one, they offer an ideal home for orchids where they can be enjoyed all the year round. You may wish to consider adding greenhouse-type benches in the conservatory. Alternatively, with a little imagination and flair for design a natural effect can be obtained by the use of tree branches or trunks to create a growing area. In this situation orchids will mix very well with other plants.

Air flow will have to be considered, and ideally the conservatory should have ventilators, or at least sliding doors to allow in fresh air and prevent overheating. Clear glass on the roof as well as the sides will probably make shading necessary (see page 65).

The floor covering will determine whether you can liberally splash water around and over the orchids as would be done in a greenhouse. If the floor is carpeted for use also as a living room, it will be necessary to incorporate humidity trays under the benches to give some humidity to the plants. Spraying should be possible; on a light and regular basis it should not cause much water to drip on to the floor.

Consideration should also be given to heating the conservatory – how much will depend upon which orchids you choose to grow. As with a cellar, it may be possible to run a further radiator from the central heating system – this should make little or no difference to your heating bill. Conservatories with double glazing will allow plants to be grown up to, and with leaves touching, the glass. This can make considerable saving where space is at a premium.

Growing orchids in a conservatory has many of the advantages of indoor growing, without restricting the size to which plants can grow. It provides a place to sit and enjoy the orchids around you, even on a cold winter night with the nearest conditions to greenhouse growing but with no need to go out to check on temperature in the late evening.

SETTING UP A SMALL GROWING AREA

Whether you are starting with a single small orchid or a little group, they should be provided with good growing conditions wherever you are keeping them. A solitary plant is unlikely to do well if isolated in an unsuitable place, so provide your single orchid with its own accompanying 'garden'. This simply means placing the plant in a humidity tray with other green plants which enjoy the same conditions. This, together with the water in the tray, will give the plant or plants the right micro-climate to encourage growth. It then only needs regular light spraying and even moisture at the roots to make the plants feel at home. If you have chosen a bright section of a conservatory some shade may be needed. This can be a shade cloth set up immediately above the plants. Do not place the orchids under the bench to keep them away from the bright sun. This avoids the direct sun, but cuts down on light as well, and the floor area can be considerably colder, taking longer to warm up during the day. Not a good place to put orchids!

A group of Cattleya *type hybrids. To be grown in a warm, light area, these and similar fragrant varieties will bloom spring and autumn. Mature plants can become quite large.*

SUMMERING OUT OF DOORS

Many orchids can be grown out of doors for the summer. However, if your orchids are growing and flowering satisfactorily where they are, there should be no need to move them. Orchids are usually put out of doors to produce a harder growth, which in turn will make it easier for them to bloom. Therefore the plants which will benefit the most are those which have not flowered for a season or two (the reasons for non-flowering are discussed in Chapter 4). Orchids may also need to move outside if there is no suitable summer accommodation – an overheating conservatory where the temperature is uncontrolled, or perhaps their space is needed for a summer crop, such as tomatoes, which is not compatible with orchids. Apart from flowering-sized plants, young or sickly plants can benefit from being outside in a shady area. Not all orchids, however, can withstand the vigours of an summer existence outside and those not suited include the warm-growing, shade-loving phalaenopsis, paphiopedilums, and most vandas, which like the heat (the exception being *Vanda* Rothschildiana and a few others which can be grown cooler and usually bloom all the better for it). Soft-leaved plants such as lycastes may do well out of doors but will have their foliage spoiled and spotted by the wind and rain. Newly repotted plants which have not yet established new roots, and plants in flower spike should not go outside either.

These exceptions apart, most cool-growing genera will improve their growth and flowering capabilities in the outdoor conditions. Miltoniopsis and pure odontoglossums should be given plenty of shade. Cymbidiums, dendrobiums, coelogynes, encyclias and maxillarias will all benefit greatly, and after one summer in the open a change in the growth of many of them will be noted. Plumper pseudobulbs, often shorter on dendrobiums, and shorter leaves of better substance are two of the characteristic changes which take place. Cattleyas and their allied hybrids can be put out with reservation, to be brought inside only during periods of dull, wet weather. Putting the plants outside could be particularly beneficial if they are healthy but not flowering.

The orchids can go outside some time in the early summer when the danger of night frosts has passed, to be returned to the house as summer ends, when the nights begin to get colder and the overnight temperature is dropping to below 7°C (45°F).

The ideal position for the orchids would be by a fence or hedge, on a patio or grassed area which receives the morning or late afternoon and evening sun, but is shaded at midday. Benches can be set up for the plants to keep them off the ground. Small plants can have their pots plunged into a tray of gravel or peat to help keep them cool and prevent them from drying out too quickly. Top-heavy plants can have their pots placed in heavier containers to prevent damage by being blown over. Moisture trays should not be necessary, but with regular spraying and watering the plants will remain fresh. It is not a good idea to hang plants in fruit trees or place them directly underneath. Many insects, including some unwanted pests such as aphids, red spider mite and mealy bug inhabit trees and will all too readily move on to the orchids.

Orchids out of doors will require more rather than less daily attention. Once out of the controlled, gentler climate indoors, they are subjected to the elements with which the grower must keep pace. During hot dry sunny spells spraying will be needed two or three times a day. Because the water will dry up very quickly, the spraying can be really heavy, almost amounting to what would be a watering indoors. When the weather turns dull or wet, the plants may go for days without watering or spraying. It may even be necessary to protect them from continual rain by erecting a waterproof covering over them for a few days. Keep a continuous eye on the weather, to keep the orchids moist without becoming saturated. In these circumstances feeding can be somewhat hit and miss. The amount of artificial feed can be stepped up to compensate for what is washed away by rain or spray, and more frequent feeding will be needed to balance the tougher climate and extra light getting to the plants. It is surprising how quickly foliage can turn yellow when exposed to too much light, particularly if the plants have not been receiving enough beforehand. Too much exposure to bright light too quickly can cause shock to a plant which will result in the loss of some of its foliage.

Be on the lookout for slugs and snails and take precautions to prevent them getting on to the bench. When the time comes to bring the plants indoors again, check for woodlice and similar pests which get into the compost. A watering with a weak solution of Jeyes fluid should flush them out. The plants will also be in need of tidying up, some black tips may have appeared, and old bracts and broken leaves will need removing. But your plants will now be looking fitter and better than ever before and the cymbidiums should be bristling with flower spikes!

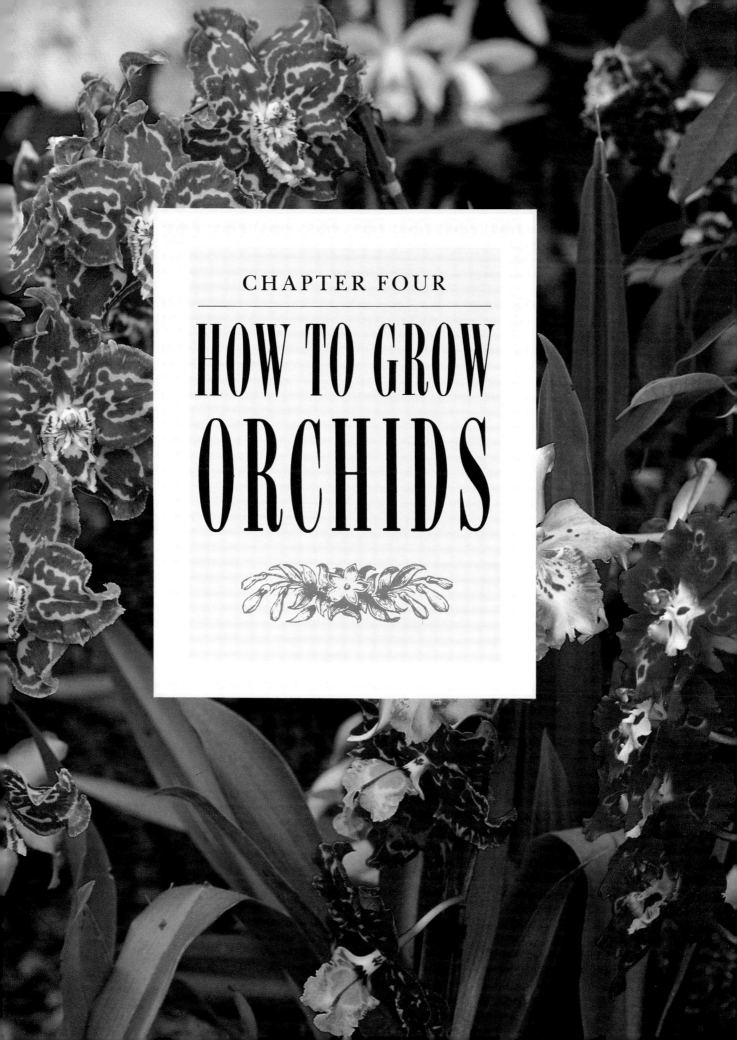

CHAPTER FOUR

HOW TO GROW
ORCHIDS

*O*rchid growing becomes easy once you have set up the right growing conditions (discussed in Chapter 3) and have acquired an understanding of how your plants grow, (discussed in Chapter 1.) From this stage on all the other aspects, such as watering and feeding, become straightforward.

SIGNS OF GOOD HEALTH

The art of orchid growing is to maintain your plants in a state of consistent good health. Far from always remaining the same, they are growing organisms in a continually changing state. Their rate of growth is not constant, they will achieve 'peaks' and 'lows' in their lifetime: some years growing forward, increasing their size and progressing well, at other times going into a slowing down period when extra coaxing is required to build them up again. This, of course, is true of many plants, not just orchids.

Good health in a plant of any age is evident first of all by the state of the pseudobulbs. Individually they should be plump, firm and green. Some shrivelling is inevitable, particularly during or just after a resting period or where a plant has a heavy flush of flowers. But this is a temporary condition, and should be for a few weeks only, after which they plump up again. The progression of pseudobulbs is important also, and it should be evident that there is a steady increase in their size from the smallest seedling pseudobulb. On mature plants, which have long since lost their earlier pseudobulbs their size should at least be maintained. Evergreen orchids should always have more pseudobulbs in leaf than out of leaf. There will come a time when this is not so, but it can be rectified at repotting by removing the surplus pseudobulbs and restoring the balance of the plant. A plant can have any number of pseudobulbs provided there are more in leaf than out of leaf. Such a plant is 'balanced' and healthy. Leaves should have an 'alert' appearance, always cool and fresh to the touch.

SIGNS OF POOR HEALTH

Pseudobulbs decreasing in size from the back (the oldest and probably leafless) to the front are struggling and the plant is growing weaker by the year. A revision of culture and possible dramatic changes in the conditions provided for the plant will be needed.

Orchids can be pulled back from the brink by improved culture. However, there comes a point where it is simply not practical to give valuable house space to a lingering plant. Often it is of greater advantage to the grower simply to discard the plant and invest in a healthy specimen to take its place. Having said that, certain orchids often have a sentimental value far greater than their monetary worth which can make a grower reluctant to give up on a favourite specimen.

Deciduous orchids can present something of a problem. A string of pseudobulbs all without their foliage would be perfectly normal for say a *lycaste* during its resting period. A *Cymbidium* in the same state would spell disaster. Provided the *Lycaste*'s pseudobulbs remain the same size or can be seen to be increasing, leave well alone; only if the latest one shows a decrease in size will it be time to remove some from the back of the plant. Some deciduous orchids have extremely short-lived pseudobulbs. The deciduous calanthes, pleiones and thunias produce pseudobulbs (or, in the case of thunias, canes) which last through two growing seasons before coming exhausted. The best way to learn about the different behaviour of your orchids is by observation of the plants. They are the best teachers.

Pseudobulbs can be affected by rot associated with poor conditions, watery swellings, premature decay, or be attacked by slugs and snails. This last is unlikely indoors, but could be a problem where plants are summered outside.

It is not always realized that orchids can suffer from stress which occurs when conditions become intolerable. This can show itself in several ways. Premature loss of foliage following rapid yellowing may occur in all the pseudobulbs bar the leading ones. Causes of such a dramatic reaction by the plant could be a sudden great change in temperature or light, or through repotting at the wrong time of year. Plants can even die from shock!

Generally, the more leaves a plant can naturally support, the better. Premature leaf loss, yellowing of foliage, even broken and damaged leaves are all signs of neglect.

THE CARE OF ORCHIDS

WATERING

The aim of watering is to keep the compost evenly moist while the plant is in an active growing state. How much water it will take to achieve this depends upon the type of compost used, the size of the pot, when the orchid was last repotted, and how many roots are in the pot. For water to penetrate to the roots, a plant in need of repotting, with roots visible around the rim which have probably pushed the plant up a centimetre ($\frac{1}{2}$ in) or so, will require perhaps double the amount of water sufficient for a recently repotted plant with maximum room in the pot. Plants in an open bark mix can have water poured liberally over the surface, as most will go straight through. A peat compost, on the other hand, would become easily saturated by this amount, and far less water can be given at one time, as more of it will be retained. When using a rockwool mix (see Chapter 5), this can be kept far wetter than other conventional composts, without killing the roots.

Either mains water or rain water can be used. Orchids like to be slightly acid, and most areas where the water is reasonably soft will suit them. If your tap water is very hard it may be better for your plants if you use rainwater, provided some method of collecting it can be easily devised. Ideally, the water should be used at room temperature, particularly for orchids growing in a warm case. Watering them with icy cold water in winter could cause the roots to become chilled.

Watering can be done with a spouted can, flooding the whole surface at one time, allowing to soak, and, if in a bark compost (see Chapter 5), flooding again. Where the plants are to be taken to the kitchen for watering, the alternative is to soak them in a bucket of water. This should not come too far over the rim otherwise some of the compost will become loose and float away.

If a plant is underwatered and so not receiving sufficient moisture for its needs, newly developing leaves will slow their growth rate, and pseudobulbs will begin to shrivel, first the older ones at the back and finally the latest ones to be formed. Underneath, the roots also will

Where only a few orchids are grown it may be better to take each plant to the sink to be watered individually. After a good soaking with the can the plant is drained and returned to its growing place.

shrivel and stop growing. Foliage will become limp and dehydrated – this is particularly noticeable on phalaenopsis and cattleyas whose leaves are broad and fleshy. At the first sign of shrivelling pseudobulbs or dehydrating foliage, if a plant is found to be very dry, it should be given a good soak for ten minutes or so, and from then on the watering increased. Within a few weeks those pseudobulbs will have plumped up again. It is easier to underwater a plant which has grown out of its pot, and as soon as this plant can be repotted, the problem will solve itself.

Overwatering occurs when too much water is given and saturation is reached and maintained over a period of time. Finally, the roots die through excessive moisture and lack of air. With the roots gone, the pseudobulbs begin to shrivel and the foliage becomes limp, exactly the same symptoms as the underwatered plant, but for the opposite reasons! The grower should not find it difficult to determine which state a plant is in. If the roots are found to be dead, the remedy is to allow the plant to dry out, and repot as soon as possible to enable the dead roots and old compost to be removed, after which new roots will soon start and this will enable the pseudobulbs to plump up again. Watering is done all year round, although most orchids require a lot less in the winter, some hardly any.

SPRAYING

Spraying is not watering. The two are separate operations, both of equal importance to the orchids. Most orchids can benefit from regular spraying for most of the year. In a conservatory, where water splashes don't matter, the orchids can be sprayed two or three times a day in spring and summer, to perhaps once a day in the winter, and not at all during very cold sunless weather. Too much winter spraying will cause the leaves to become spotted. For the same reason buds and flowers should always be kept dry. Indoors, within the confined area of a case, spraying is easy, as the excess water runs to the water tray below. It may create a problem if plants standing on the window sill are constantly sprayed. At best the spray will have to be very light, just sufficient to allow droplets of water to sit on the leaf like dew. Other green plants around the orchids can also be sprayed. An alternative method of keeping leaves fresh and free from dust is to wipe each leaf daily with a wet sponge or tissue. This is obviously more time-consuming, and there is always the danger of cracking or splitting a leaf, so it is only practical where a very limited number of plants are being grown.

Spraying is essential for freshening up aerial roots such as may be made on plants growing in a case, and to some extent will take over from watering of plants growing on bark. It is also useful for rapid cooling of leaves in summer, should the conservatory become overheated on a hot day.

Cymbidiums are perhaps the toughest of orchids and can be sprayed generously. *Odontoglossum* types, coelogynes, dendrobiums, maxillarias and encyclias, are a few which like light spraying, while those with much softer leaves are better sprayed infrequently or not at all. These include cattleyas, masdevallias, zygopetalums and lycastes. Their leaves will all too easily become spotted through water remaining on them for too long. Paphiopedilums and phalaenopsis may be very lightly sprayed if there is a small fan incorporated in their case to ensure they dry off quickly. Otherwise the leaves can be occasionally wiped over.

Most days spraying can be done in the morning, when the room is getting warmer. If it is sunny, spray again at midday or in early afternoon. A third spray may be given in summer during the longest days. Plants growing under artificial lights can be sprayed the same all the year round, provided they dry off well before the lights go out.

FEEDING

It is always stated that in their natural environment orchids are weak feeders, their very existence perched on the branches of trees allows that they do not need a rich source of nutrients. However, we know that in the wild their roots will travel long distances (often more than 1 m or 3 ft) over rough bark or even inside rotting trees where there must be some nutrients available. The rich humus from decaying leaves which collects in the axils of branches also provides some orchids with a good food supply. At one time it was thought that orchids lived entirely on water and air, and the feeding of them was considered very unwise. Today, feeding is known to be as important to their state of health as watering, and there are a number of feeds available made exclusively for orchids. These are suited to the orchids' low but continuous rate of growth over many years. Feeding becomes more important where an inert rockwool type of compost is used (see Chapter 5) as it is simply a medium for growing roots; the minerals have to be added. If one of the specially designed orchid feeds is not available, use any of the more popular feeds that cater for a range of plants, using it at the most diluted rate usually recommended for ornamental plants. Some manufacturers produce two orchid feeds, one nitrogen-based and one phosphate-based, to be used consecutively throughout most of the year, the first to promote good growth and the latter to encourage flowering. If using this type of liquid fertilizer do not give more than the recommended dose. There are also different kinds of slow-release fertilizer for house-plants in the form of pellets or sticks, which can also be used for orchids provided they are used *very* sparingly. The advantage of liquid feed is that when diluted it can be used to water the plants with, thus getting straight to the roots, or it can be sprayed (where this is possible) on to the leaves to be taken up directly by them. Spraying leaves is of benefit where the foliage has become yellow due to the need for repotting or loss of roots. Foliar spraying to include aerial roots is a must for plants growing without pots. Those orchids whose foliage is better kept dry, such as lycastes, miltonias, paphiopedilums and pleiones, are better given feed to their pot, and feed sprayed on orchids growing outside may quickly be washed off by rain. Newly repotted plants are better sprayed until they have produced new roots to take up the feed.

Artificial feeding generally commences early in the year, about once a fortnight, or every third watering. As the spring growth approaches its period of maximum activity the feed can be increased to every other watering or once a week for the summer period. As autumn approaches reduce to the early spring amount and for those orchids still growing give a feed every three weeks throughout the winter. Resting orchids which will be left dry need no feeding after watering has ceased until they start again in the new year. Plants growing under artificial light can have extra feed during the winter to balance the extra light they are getting. Basically, the more light reaching the plants, the more feed can be given, as orchids respond to light with faster growth and can convert more food into energy.

RESTING

The period between the completion of the pseudobulb and the commencement of the next new growth from that pseudobulb is termed the resting period. This is a time of inactivity during which the plant remains dormant. In the wild this enables the plant to cope with the dry season which may last for many weeks, during which little or no rain may reach it. In cultivation, this rest period mostly, but not always, occurs in the winter. A few orchids will rest in the summer or at other times. When an orchid goes to rest it may or may not lose its leaves, its root tips cease to grow and become enclosed by the velamen. Its pseudobulbs remain plump or shrivel slightly during its rest. The resting period can vary from a few weeks to several months. Cymbidiums, odontoglossums and miltoniopsis are examples of evergreen orchids with very short resting periods, during which they are usually flowering. The new growth follows immediately after flowering, so the grower does not usually realize the plant is resting and it needs no alteration to its routine culture. Coelogynes, encyclias and maxillarias are among the evergreen orchids which take a longer rest, and a drying out period is necessary for them during the winter. Deciduous orchids, which include many of the dendrobiums, lycastes and the cooler growing pleiones, also have a lengthened rest. There are other genera which choose to go to rest in the summer and grow throughout the winter. Phalaenopsis do not have a noticeable rest: one leaf follows another in a continuous succession, although growth does slow down in the winter months. Paphiopedilums behave similarly, starting a new growth almost immediately after the completion and flowering of the previous one. Many orchids take the opportunity while they are not growing of producing their flower spikes. This means flowers and growth are not being produced at the same time.

By early winter most orchids which are going to rest will have completed and matured their pseudobulbs. The deciduous ones will drop their leaves. Some evergreen types may lose a leaf or two from the back of the plant, others will shed them in the spring, just prior to the new growing season. By gradually lessening the water, by the end of the year the plants will be quite dry. In a greenhouse where there is always some humid air the plants can be kept much drier than indoors where there is little or no humidity. Here some water will be needed to prevent the orchids from shrivelling. This may mean an occasional watering every three weeks or so. Provided the pseudobulbs remain plump even this may not be needed. Much will depend upon how much water was given during the previous summer and whether the plant was able to

Cymbidiums will grow and flower on a light window sill area. In this situation they should be kept moist all the year round, and lightly sprayed once or twice a day.

hold sufficient reserves of water for the winter. Underwatering during the summer will make it difficult to rest the plant properly in winter.

At any time in the new year the first of the resting orchids will show their new growths, and new movement will begin. From this stage watering can be resumed and a little later on, say after two or three weeks, feeding can also recommence.

FLOWERING

The ultimate aim of growing orchids is to bring them into flower. In their natural environment it is essential for the continuation of the species that blooming occurs regularly. The conditions under which the plants grow promote flowering by encouraging the embryo flower spike into activity. This is one reason why we strive to imitate these conditions as near as possible in our homes. How well we succeed is borne out by how well our plants bloom. Many of the orchids we cultivate are mountain plants coming from altitudes of up to 1500 m (5000 ft) or so, where the atmosphere is quite different. It is this altitude which is impossible to recreate in our homes. Nevertheless, when all other aspects of their culture are right, as previously described, blooming will follow as a matter of course.

Cymbidiums and *Odontoglossum* types are examples of plants which produce their flower spikes at the end of the growing season, as the pseudobulb nears completion. The flower spike comes from the base of the newly completed pseudobulb, from inside the first basal leaf. The growing spike will take about six weeks to produce its flowers. Orchids can be expected to bloom in their third or fourth year, after which they should bloom annually. Cymbidiums will bloom at the same time each year, growing and flowering on a twelve-month cycle. The *Odontoglossum*- bred genera such as *Vuylstekeara* grow on a nine- or ten-monthly cycle and will therefore often bloom at a different time each year. Look for the flower spikes as the pseudobulb matures and before the next growth starts. All being well the plants will bloom and then start their new growth after the old flower spike has been cut. Once the new growth has started, the pseudobulb behind it will not bloom again. If the new growth starts before a flower spike appears, that pseudobulb will not bloom. Cymbidiums often produce new growths at the same time as their flowers spikes, one coming from either side of the pseudobulb and looking identical at first. As they grow the new growth fans out into a spray of leaves, while the flower spike, which is fatter, grows to resemble a pencil, eventually showing buds emerging from the protective sheath. At this stage they may need to be supported by a cane to prevent snapping or bending too low. Support the spike to the base of the buds and leave it to form an arch (some will remain upright). *Cymbidium* blooms will last for up to eight weeks.

Cattleyas and their hybrids bloom from the top of their pseudobulbs. As the new growth advances a sheath can be seen between the leaves (or beside a single leaf) which, when the pseudobulb matures, protects the young buds which develop inside. When large enough they push their way out through the sheath which splits along its edge to allow them to emerge. The sheath then dries up and turns brown. Sometimes this may happen before the buds emerge, and it may be necessary to snip off the top to ensure the buds get safely through. Cattleyas may bloom during the spring or autumn; often they have two growing cycles a year, thereby blooming twice. They too tend to bloom at the same time each year. If the plants are kept slightly cooler and drier while in bloom, the flowers will last longer, up to three or four weeks.

Encyclias also bloom from the top of their pseudobulbs. Not all produce sheaths, and the small buds can be watched as they grow and develop into flowers. Coelogynes mainly bloom from within the centre of the new growth, the flower spike coming from between the new leaves and growing at a faster rate so as to bloom free of the foliage. There are variations to this among the different species. Zygopetalums also produce flower spikes from the base of the new growth, but bloom at the start of the growing season rather than at the end of it.

Dendrobiums bloom from the completed pseudobulb or cane in various ways. The *D. nobile* types and hybrids produce flowers in ones and twos for most of their length, the buds emerging from the nodes opposite the base of the leaf – or where the leaf was, as generally it is the older leafless canes which bloom. A cane which does not bloom one year can do so the next if conditions are improved, so the grower need not lose out, but will get more than one season's flowers at a single blooming! Other dendrobiums, *D. infundibulum*, for example, blooms from the top of the canes only, producing a large head of bloom which comes from two or three nodes. Others produce long trusses of bloom instead of one or two flowers. Most are spring-flowering, but may vary their flowering time if conditions are different. They are usually flowering from the previous summer's growth at the same time as their new growth starts from the base. Most dendrobiums have a good dry rest in the winter, which helps to promote the growth of buds in the spring. If they are not sufficiently rested, or are kept too warm during this period, the buds will be replaced by adventitious growths, which is a good way of propagating, but not of producing flowers!

Phalaenopsis produce their flower spikes from the base of the plant, alternative and opposite to the new roots, which they at first resemble. As they grow and turn upward they can be identified as flower spikes. Phalaenopsis do not have a regular flowering season, they will bloom almost every time they have made a new leaf, and they are just about the only orchids in cultivation which can become almost perpetual-blooming, often with more than one flower spike in bloom at any time. As if this were not reward enough, they are also unqiue among the cultivated orchids in that when their flower spike is cut back to a lower node once the top blooms have died, an extension to the flower spike will grow and produce even more flowers. There is a danger that these plants will flower themselves to death, and it may become necessary to remove flower spikes if no new leaves are being made at the same time. Phalaenopsis which do not bloom are most likely being grown too warm. A drop in temperature for a period of just three to four weeks will no doubt have the desired effect.

The main reasons for the cool-growing orchids not blooming are too high a temperature at night, or too little light. Both these problems can be overcome by summering outside. Alternatively, a plant may not be in a fit enough state to bloom. Check that there are more pseudobulbs in leaf than out of leaf, and that they have not been decreasing in size. The remedy may be to repot in the spring, removing some old pseudobulbs to give the plant a fresh start. Deciduous orchids (dendrobiums, lycastes etc.) are exceptions to the pseudobulbs in leaf because only the leading one will carry foliage, but if too many are retained on the plant they may begin to lose size, so divide in spring.

KEEPING PLANTS CLEAN AND TIDY

Orchids should look as if they are *cared for*. Indoors the leaves will gather dust and a regular wiping over with a plant wet wipe once a week or so will not only keep the leaves clean and healthy, but also free from pests. Any red spider mite will show up far more easily on a white tissue. To keep your cymbidiums looking good, the old bracts covering the pseudobulbs can be removed when they have become dry after the leaves have been shed. This will aid appearance and to enable more light to get to the ageing pseudobulb. The bract is removed carefully without damaging the base of the pseudobulb by splitting the halves of bract down each side of the pseudobulb and gently pulling away. If this has not been done to a plant for a number of years, it is surprising how much neater it will look.

Old flower spikes should be cut off at the base, and any supporting canes removed, together with old string ties.

RECOGNIZING COMMON PROBLEMS

All too often it is only when an orchid has not bloomed for a number of years that we begin to question whether it is in a healthy state. It is natural for all orchids to bloom annually, or upon completion of a season's growth. Orchids which do not bloom are being prevented from doing so by the conditions under which they are growing. First look at the plant to see whether it is in a fit state to bloom. All the points mentioned already – including shrivelled or diminishing pseudobulbs, too much loss of leaf or limp foliage – will render the plant too weak to bloom. In these cases some adjustments to the culture will be needed. The best course of action would be to wait until the spring, and repot the plant into fresh compost. After taking a good look at the environment provided you should be able to decide what can be done to improve the growing conditions for the plants.

Orchids which appear in all the above aspects to be fit and well, and therefore capable of blooming, but still do not produce flowers, are probably suffering from an inbalance in their culture. The most common causes are either too high a temperature, producing a soft lazy plant, or too low a temperature, which has slowed down the growth so that flowering is impaired. On the other hand, an absolutely *constant* temperature is not good for plant growth either. Only in caves do we find a constant temperature and orchids do not grow in caves! There should be a reasonable fluctuation between day and night temperature – even in the tropics the nights can be very cold.

Light also can be crucial to the flowering of orchids. We talk about the ripening of pseudobulbs and giving extra light at the end of summer to achieve this, but it is not always easy to define this ripening. Many fruits dramatically change colour as they ripen, so the grower can see when they are ready to be picked. Not so with orchids. We can only note a slight change in leaf colour and hope our pseudobulbs are ripening fully. Only when the flower spike appears can we be sure that an individual plant has received enough light. As the light requirement can vary from plant to plant, experience through careful observation will enable you to aquire the skill to bring into bloom regularly a variety of plants. This is all part of the fulfilment of orchid growing.

To increase the light may involve moving the plant to another position altogether, either within the house or conservatory, or even out of doors on to the patio for the duration of the summer.

Orchid leaves are healthier and look better when regularly cleaned to remove dust and dirt. Also, any insect pests will more easily show up after gently wiping a white tissue along the leaf.

The loss of roots, other than naturally, is an all too common problem, caused either by overwatering, underwatering or a soured or otherwise unacceptable compost. Different composts will have different water capacity; some need less water than others. Orchids which have suffered the loss of all or most of a root system should be allowed to remain on the dry side until the spring repotting time, when a fresh and possibly dryer compost could be used. In the meantime regular but light spraying, or wiping of the foliage will prevent further moisture loss through the leaves. Dehydration must be prevented if the plant is to be kept going until repotting and the commencement of new roots.

PESTS AND DISEASES

Plants indoors have the advantage of growing in isolated conditions, maintaining little contact with the outside world; this means that they are not generally troubled with the typical pests. Plants growing in a garden are subjected to a continual bombardment from a variety of insect pests which have to be constantly combated with insecticides to protect the plants. Greenhouse plants are likewise affected, often more so as the artificially warm conditions created for them also provide an ideal habitat for garden pests. Every type of pest, from slugs and snails to greenfly and red spider mite, can establish itself in the greenhouse from the garden outside.

In the home the plants are separated from all these problems, and there should be no need to resort to the modern chemical insecticides. Because they can be dangerous and quite unsuitable for use indoors, insecticides are not recommended for orchids in the home. Far safer, and often just as effective, is a box of tissues and plenty of clean water.

Ideally you should start with clean healthy plants, and provided your orchids have been obtained from a reliable source, the plants should be free from any insect pests.

GREENFLY

By their nature orchids do not make very good hosts for a variety of predators; Their tough foliage makes them undesirable to many of the common or garden pests. Greenfly could possibly gain acess to your orchids during the summer through open windows, but even so they seldom attack orchid leaves, except some of the varieties with the most delicate annual foliage, or possibly tender young growths. If greenfly are apparent, they will almost certainly be found on the young buds or flowers. Regular inspection of developing buds will soon detect this pest which is not difficult to see with the naked eye. The greenfly is a sap-sucking predator which pierces the surface of the buds, causing deform-ity of the cells which becomes more pronounced as the buds become larger. When the flower opens it is greatly disfigured, with blotching and twisting of the sepals and petals. If the greenfly attack has been severe and unchecked the buds will turn yellow and drop off without opening. These aphids have one of the fastest breeding rates of all insects and they spread quickly, building up into colonies if not controlled.

At the first sign of a few greenfly it is sufficient to wipe them off between finger and thumb or with a wad of cotton wool. If the greenfly can be seen in and around a tight cluster of buds too small to be handled, they may be dislodged with the aid of a small paint brush. Alternatively, the buds can be immersed in a bowl of water and swilled gently round until the pest is dislodged. The water should be used at room temperature, and the surplus shaken from the buds. This method is far better where just a few aphids are noticed than immediate spraying with insecticide which can damage soft buds.

RED SPIDER MITE

Red spider mite is well known to any gardener. It will attack a whole range of plants outdoors and in the greenhouse. It is a most persistent and extremely small mite which usually requires a magnifying glass to see it at all. The mites are roundish and pale yellowish orange. Breathing on the leaf to warm it will speed their movement so they can be spotted. On orchids they will first attack the undersides of the leaves where a silvery pattern can be detected on the surface. This is caused by the mite piercing the leaf, killing the leaf cells, and these areas will spread if the pest remains undetected. Eventually, the white areas turn brown and black as a result of secondary infection feeding on the dead leaf cells.

The best method of prevention and control indoors is regular sponging of the leaves using a moist white paper tissue. On cymbidiums the leaf should be supported at its base with one hand, while the tissue is run the length of the leaf held between finger and thumb. Inspection of the tissue will reveal any red spider mite, although you may need the help of a magnifying glass.

SCALE INSECTS AND MEALY BUG

Two further pests which are traditionally troublesome to orchids are scale insects and mealy bug. These are usually introduced into a collection on freshly imported species and sometimes remain undetected, concealed beneath sheaths of cattleyas and similar orchids. The scale insect is as its common name describes: it may be round or oval and usually lives in clusters on the less accessible parts of the plant. The mealy bug is white, and covers itself in a powdery substance. It frequents similar parts of the plant as the scale insect. Both these pests are large enough to be seen with the naked eye, although they may have to be searched for, especially around the base of the plant. They both thrive in a dry atmosphere and can build up into large colonies. If allowed to go unchecked they will slowly sap the strength of the plant, weakening it and eventually causing its death. These pests can be all too easily missed when sponging the leaves, and in searching for them, the old leaf bracts covering the pseudobulbs should be carefully removed by slitting and peeling back. The best method of control is to take a small artist's brush dipped in a solution of methylated spirit and liberally paint the areas suspected of harbouring the pests. Methylated spirits kills the soft, unprotected mealy bug upon contact and its swift penetrating action will find those which remain unseen. Scale insects, particularly the hard, mussel type, must be dislodged to be killed, and the best method of removing any visible scale is by scrubbing with an old tooth brush dipped in methylated spirit. This treatment will not harm the base of the plant in any way, but if spirit is used on the leaves they should be immediately washed with clean water. On very soft-leaved orchids methylated spirits can cause some burning, and it should never be used on flower buds for the same reason. In any case, this should not become necessary as these pests are unlikely to be found on the faster developing flowers spikes and buds.

VIRUS AND FUNGAL INFECTIONS

There are not many diseases which affect orchids. Those which do include the viruses which will usually attack plants which have become weakened from poor health. Virus in cymbidiums will show up as black diamond-shaped flecking along part or all of the leaf surface. There is no known cure for this virus, although it can be arrested if growing conditions are improved. Red spider mite will transmit virus from one plant to another – another reason to keep this pest at bay. Other marks in the form of black patches, tips or spots are more than likely cultural problems and can be prevented by improved conditions.

Virus in phalaenopsis will appear as blackened pitted areas sometimes resulting in loss of the leaf or the whole plant. Plants which appear to have virus should be grown in isolation, or thrown out.

Fungal spots can occur on foliage or flowers due to faulty conditions, usually a combination of low temperatures combined with too much watering or spraying near the blooms. When they break out on foliage or pseudobulbs, forming watery swellings, a powdered fungicide mixed with water to make a paste can be generously applied to the affected area. The skin of the swellings can first be broken to release the water inside.

RECUPERATING PLANTS

Plants may become sick for a number of reasons, usually associated with unsuitable growing conditions or neglect. Because orchids are so resilient they are hard to kill and a neglected plant can remain in a state of poor health, even flowering, for many years, constantly trying to recuperate with new growths which may or may not reach maturity.

Neglect usually leads to poor health when a plant is not being repotted regularly on a two-year basis. Once the pot has been crammed to overflowing with pseudobulbs and all available pot space occupied by roots, both dead and alive, the plant can no longer prosper. To reduce energy output the plant sheds leaves, and premature leaf loss may entail the loss of some or all foliage. This leaves a collection of leafless pseudobulbs which will produce greatly weakened new growths. Repotting at this stage can save the life of the plant, splitting up the pseudobulbs and potting them singly. These pseudobulbs will, with improved growing conditions, require at least two or three years before they reach flowering stage once again. Neglected plants which have been rescued from an outside source should also be checked for virus disease, which so often attacks weak and ailing plants. If this can be seen to be in any remaining foliage it would be better not to grow the plants alongside those already in your collection. A sick plant which needs careful growing for several years before flowering may be taking up valuable space which could be occupied by a more rewarding plant and it would have to be a very special plant to be tolerated for years without blooming. On the other hand, provided the neglected plant appears to be free from virus disease, it can be a rewarding challenge for the grower to bring it back to a state of good health.

The worst thing to befall a monopodial orchid is for it is lose its centre. Probably through water getting into the top axil, the top dies and the centre leaf rots. Not all is lost provided the 'crown' of the plant is not affected. If the plant is treated with sulphur to stop the rot spreading and kept on the dry side, new growth will almost certainly grow from the base, or if a vanda, from partway up the rhizome. Phalaenopsis can become completely defoliated, by cold or some other cultural problem, but retain live roots and, if given improved conditions, will grow again from the base. A plant like this can then be treated as a propagation.

If your own plants are growing well, it is easier to recuperate a plant arriving in a sick state, but if your own plants are showing the symptoms of neglect, take a good look at the conditions you are providing to see where you have gone wrong. Some dramatic changes in the plant's life style may be called for, and if it is not obvious to you where you may have gone wrong, this would be a good time to visit your nearest orchid nursery with the sick plants to seek advice. When a nurseryman can see your plants he will in all probability be able to tell you what has gone wrong. This is if the plant you show him is still alive, but there is little point in taking along a dead plant to show as all one can say is that it is dead, and it may not be easy to determine the cause of death once it has happened.

In the event of some catastrophe, a fire in the vicinity of the plants, or a power failure resulting in plants suffering from cold, for example, the extent of the damage will show within a week. Burnt or chilled leaves will turn black and drop off, but those plants with pseudobulbs may be saved. The pseudobulbs are tougher than the leaves and may not be affected. If they are, they will turn brown and soft quite quickly. Once you can see how much of the plant is unaffected, repotting is again the answer, removing all dead portions, and reducing the plant to propagated segments to be grown on once again to flowering size.

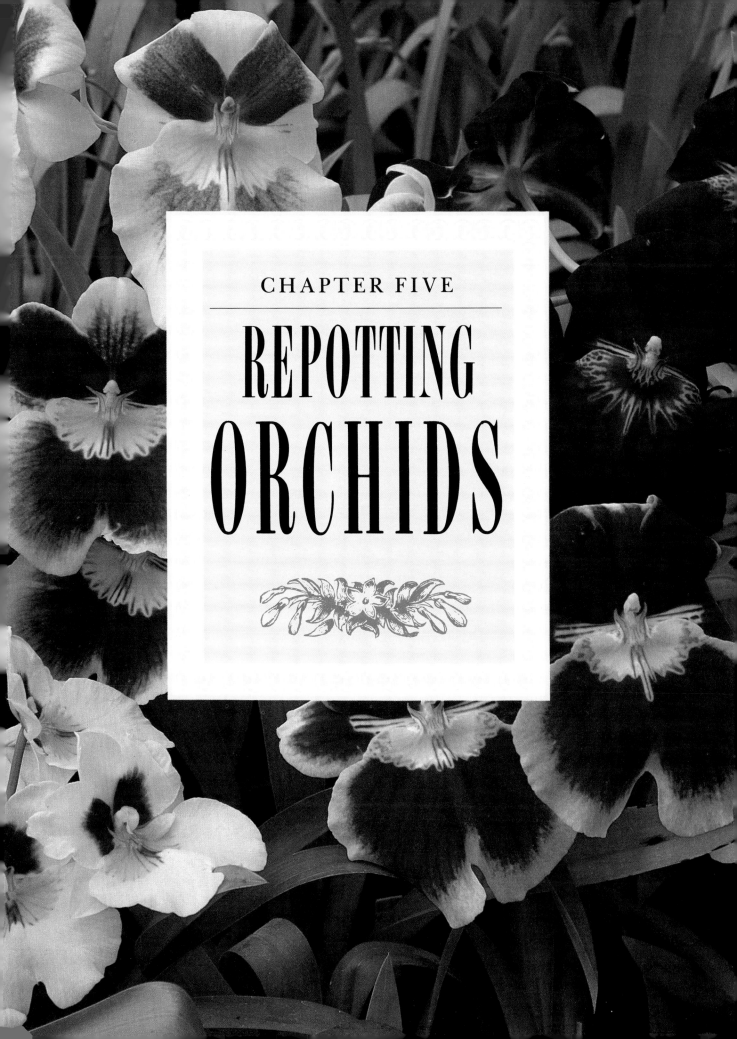

CHAPTER FIVE
REPOTTING
ORCHIDS

*T*n their natural state orchid roots will meander along tree branches, inside hollow trunks, or over mossy rocks for several metres or many feet, constantly seeking out the meagre nutrients required for their long existence. These same roots confined to the limitations of a pot will wind their roots round and round until all space is used up, and all the food value in the compost is exhausted. Artificial feed can be supplemented, but as the compost ages and breaks down so it needs to be replaced on a regular basis. Also, orchids increase in size, and as they outgrow one pot they should be moved on to another larger size. If done correctly at the right time of the year, repotting causes no setbacks to a plant and should not interfere with its next season's flowering.

> *To achieve an ongoing state of growth, regular repotting is advisable. Most adult plants will need repotting every other year, some may go longer. Young plants, seedlings growing on from flasks, or propagations will need repotting or 'dropping on' about every six months or so to keep them progressing well. This time is lengthened to twelve months as they get older, and finally every other year when the plant is adult at about five years of age.*

WHEN TO REPOT

Repotting is best done in the spring. The plant will tell you when: look for the new spring growth which can appear at any time once the days begin to lengthen. Ideally, when the new growth is several centimetres or a few inches high you should repot. At this stage the plant, which may have been resting throughout the winter, will be on the move again, and will be approaching its period of maximum activity. New roots always follow new growth, therefore you should repot before these start. By the time growth has speeded up in early summer, the new roots will be able to take advantage of the fresh compost.

Try not to disturb a plant once its growing season is well under way. This will cause unnecessary shock to the whole system, with damage to and possible loss of the roots, resulting in an abnormal slowing down of growth. By the end of the summer, when temperatures slacken and daylight hours lessen, the growth rate will begin to slow naturally as pseudobulbs mature. Those orchids which continue to grow throughout the winter, albeit more slowly, may be repotted at this time. The cooler nights before the winter sets in will often produce an extra spurt of growth and new roots. At this time repotting or 'dropping on' (page 95) will do no harm. The plant will have time to settle down before winter. Midwinter is not a good time to disturb any plant because of its slow rate of growth; it is taking up little or nothing from the compost and could take a long time to recover, causing early shrivelling of pseudo-bulbs to the detriment of new growth in spring.

The above are general guidelines on when to repot the majority of orchids. However, the formation of new roots can take preference over the time of year. If a plant in need of repotting has noticeable new growth, it is about to make new roots. Unless this is midwinter, repot as soon as possible. This happens because some orchids will take, say, nine months to complete their season's growth and will therefore be growing (and flowering) at a different time each year.

An orchid is in need of repotting when its growth has filled the pot and there is no room for any more pseudobulbs or growths. Alternatively, the plant may have so many roots crowded into the pot that it has pushed itself up above the pot rim, making it very difficult to water. The thicker rooting orchids – cymbidiums, zygopetalums and cattleyas – tend to do this. The foliage may be growing paler, which is a sign that the compost is used up. If the compost has become so loose that you can push a finger through it, that is also an indication that it has decomposed considerably. Repot also if a plant has become sickly; probably it has lost its roots, and stale or sour compost may be the cause. Repot also if a newly acquired plant is in a compost that you are not familiar with.

COMPOSTS

Over the 200 years or so that orchids have been cultivated many different composts have been tried out. Eventually, one or two basic types are settled upon which then last for a few decades until fashion decrees that a new compost is needed and once again the search is on for a better orchid compost. This is by no means a bad thing, but it does emphasize that orchids will grow in a wide and varied mixture of composts, all of them alien to their natural medium.

Various composts have come and gone, while many new ideas are still being tried out, some of these extremely successfully. It is, however, the basic composts which have stood the test of time that are best adhered to by the amateur indoor grower. Composts which suit large commercial establishments do not always adapt well to the very different culture of orchids indoors. Some composts can be used with great success by those who, after years of experience, have acquired a sound basic knowledge of their plants' needs, and can combine an inert compost with a well-balanced feeding programme with excellent results. Likewise, commercial establishments growing a very limited number of varieties can use a compost suited to their specific needs, but which will not necessarily suit all orchids. The average indoor grower, therefore, needs a compost suitable for a variety of orchids.

BARK

Because most orchids are descended from epiphytic species, they need an open, well-drained and durable compost, which is soil free. Probably the most widely used is bark. This is the bark from the Scotch, Corsican or similar non-resinous pine which is durable and slow to decompose. Various barks are sold for other purposes such as surfacing on garden paths, or as a mulch on flower beds. These are not suitable for orchids because they are already in a decomposing state, or are simply not of the right grade or type. That sold as 'orchid bark' by specialist nurseries should be used, often available in more than one grade, to suit different orchids. Sometimes other ingredients may have been added which are considered to be an advantage by the supplier. These additional items may include sphagnum moss or Finnish peat, perlag or charcoal, all of which have some value.

PEAT

Sphagnum or Finnish peat are both widely used for orchids and are available from most garden centres. This is a denser material than bark, and is used loosely, the peat being poured around the plant and settled

Repotting a Cymbidium ('dropping on' without disturbing the root ball).

An orchid is in need of repotting when its pseudobulbs have filled the pot and there is no room for further growth, or when the plant has pushed itself up by its roots. The best time for repotting is in spring when new growth is showing.

A healthy root system shows a ball of live white roots which has penetrated the compost to the bottom of the pot. A root system like this need not be disturbed and the plant merely needs to be put into a larger pot with all present roots intact.

A plastic pot approximately 5 cm (2 in) larger should be chosen and the plant positioned on top of a thin layer of crocks. This should allow room for two more years' growth. It may be necessary to position the plant to one side, depending on which way it is growing.

Compost (orchid bark is used here) is poured into the pot and firmed with the fingers. It is not necessary to use a potting stick for this. By pushing against the rim of the pot, no damage will be done to the roots or new growths.

without pressing down too firmly, Usually, polystyrene granules, expanded clay pellets or foam rubber chips are incorporated to keep the mix open and to aid swift drainage. Alternatively, a coarse grade of bark can be added to serve the same purpose.

SPHAGNUM MOSS

Fresh sphagnum moss, the large fluffy kind, not to be confused with 'florist's' or 'wreath' moss, is a lovely additive to peat or bark, provided it is used in a fresh state. To obtain this, you need to be able to gather your own supply. After a little time the sphagnum moss will grow on the surface of the compost, giving a very pleasant green appearance to your plants. Artificial feeding, however, may prevent this growth. Other mosses and lichens which grow on the surface of composts are not so desirable and should be removed as they will smother the surface, preventing aeration and making watering difficult.

OTHER MATERIALS

Orchids are no longer purchased only from specializing nurseries who can discuss composts with you. The main superstores and garden centres have them for sale, mostly at Christmas time when they make delightful gifts. They are usually restricted to a very few kinds, cymbidiums and phalaenopsis being the most common. These plants, which represent extremely good value, are usually found to be growing in a 'compost' of rockwool (the roofing insulation material) or oasis (as used by flower arrangers). Both these inert materials are used merely to provide a base into which the plant can send its roots. The plant relies entirely upon the nutrients put into the growing medium for its continued growth and well-being. Stop, reduce or largely alter this carefully balanced, scientifically prepared feeding programme and the plant suffers. You really need to know what balanced feed the plant has been receiving in order to continue to produce the same rate of growth from the plant for years to come. As with buying a pedigree puppy from a reputable breeder, it is an advantage to be given a diet sheet which will ensure the continued well-being of that puppy.

When purchasing orchids in one of these inert materials, if at all unsure, feed well and at the earliest opportunity it might be as well for the inexperienced grower to repot into a bark mix which will be easier to cope with. Allow at least twelve months for the plant to adjust and re-establish itself in the new compost. For the experienced grower, rockwool or oasis should pose no problems whatsoever.

Whichever compost is decided upon, it is advisable to use just one, albeit in varying grades to suit the different orchids, rather than have all your plants in a mixture of composts requiring different treatment. This is easier said than done, because most growers like to produce their own individual mix, so orchid composts vary considerably. If plants are added to your collection in vastly different materials, repot them into your favourite mix as soon as it is practical from the plant's point of view, bearing in mind the best potting time is in the spring.

For the purpose of this book, which is intended to keep to the basics, merely guiding the beginner along a path which will lead to good orchid-growing techniques, we are recommending bark compost. This is, in our opinion, by far the best compost for the beginner, being the easiest to cope with when everything else is as yet unfamiliar. All epiphytic orchids will grow well in bark; it has everything conducive to a good rooting system and a contented plant. While terrestrial orchids will also grow in bark, those such as pleiones do better in Finnish peat mixed with polystyrene granules.

When plants look poor, all too often the compost is blamed, in fact it is far more likely that it is the growing conditions or the culture which is at fault. Rapid, experimental changing from one compost to another is not recommended at an early stage. The time to do this is when you have gained sufficient knowledge to know what, if anything, is wrong with a particular compost, and why a change would be for the better. Continual and too frequent repotting using a variety of composts is an all too common mistake, creating more problems in not allowing plants time to adapt and settle down.

R E C E P T A C L E S   F O R   O R C H I D S

Orchids have been tried in all manner of receptacles, from specially made clay pots to baskets and coconut shells. In the past, when clay pots were in fashion, hand-made ones had extra holes around the edges when it was recognized that orchids like their roots to wander free from the confines of the pot. Orchids thrived in them for many years, but today they are a rarity. Plastic or polyurethane pots have proved to be just as successful, preferably shallow or half-pots.

Netted pots designed for water plants are ideal for many orchids, particularly the smaller growing species, while the larger specimens can be accommodated in ornamental hanging baskets. A disadvantage here is that these baskets are rounded at the bottom and will not stand up. Standing them inside a large flat-bottomed pot defeats the object of allowing the roots some air. Specific orchid baskets are made from a variety of hard woods and come in various sizes from most orchid nurseries. These can be suspended where space allows and are ideal for those orchids which need plenty of light such as oncidiums, laelias and other species, including the stanhopeas whose flower spikes grow downward through the compost.

Ornamental pots for large specimen plants of cymbidiums and cattleyas can greatly enhance the beauty of the plant and, particularly when it is not in flower, can make an attractive feature. Solid pots are best for thick-rooted orchids which include cymbidiums, zygopetalums and cattleyas. Many of the epiphytic species will grow extremely well mounted on pieces of bark, but this type of culture is only possible where the plants can be regularly sprayed or benefit from humidity created by, for example, an indoor ornamental pool. Orchids on bark are ideal for an indoor growing case with controlled humidity.

Some crocking for the base of the pot is necessary. Mostly used are polystyrene pieces, which are available as a waste material, or made by breaking up unwanted polystyrene. Suitably sized stones are ideal for dendrobiums which can otherwise become top heavy.

R E P O T T I N G   P R O C E D U R E S

'DROPPING ON'

This is the easiest method of repotting into a larger pot and involves the minimum of disturbance to the plant. It is therefore a good way for the beginner to become acquainted with repotting, gaining confidence and experience without the risk of causing undue harm.

Orchids can be 'dropped on' provided that the same compost is being used as that which a plant is already growing in. It would be a mistake to mix two different composts in the same pot because the watering requirements for each could vary. The compost the plant is growing in should be in good condition, it should smell sweet, and should not be too decomposed. The root system should be in good condition, without any dead roots showing on the outside of the root ball. Pseudobulbs, also, can be looked at. If there are not more in leaf than out of leaf, some need to be removed. Seedlings or young propagations will benefit greatly from being 'dropped on' regularly about every six months for two to three years. Because 'dropping on' causes little or no disturbance to the plant, it can be done at almost any time of the year, the spring and autumn months being preferable.

A plant ready for dropping on may not necessarily have filled its pot completely with growth above, but the compost may well have become a solid ball of roots, which is determined when the plant is removed from the pot. An experienced eye can tell just by looking at the state of the leaves and pseudobulbs exactly what lies below. The plant should be in a fairly dry state.

You should have ready a work area with sufficient fresh compost, which has been wetted previously, and so is in a nice damp condition, a few pots of the appropriate size, plus a quantity of crocking material.

Most orchids are easily removed by first squeezing the pot or rolling it between the hands. This should loosen the roots, which nearly always adhere to the side of the pot. Another method with heavy plants is to tap the edge of the pot against the side of the bench or table where you are working, taking care not to damage any new growth close to the pot rim. If this is the first time you have seen the roots of a particular plant, this is a good opportunity to become aquainted with them and to take a good look!

The new pot should be approximately 5 cm (2 in) larger than the previous one, which will allow just sufficient room for new growth. Place sufficient crocking in the pot to cover the base, then add a little compost on top. Remove any pieces of old crocking from the base of the root ball, and without any further disturbance to the plant, place it in the pot with the oldest pseudobulbs or growth against the rim of the pot, allowing the maximum space between the front, leading pseudobulb or growth and the pot rim. The base of the new growth should now be level with, or slightly below (but not above) the top of the pot. Hold the plant in this position and fill in all the space with compost, pouring it in and pressing down firmly with the fingers against the rim of the pot and away from the plant. Take care around the back of the plant to leave no gaps, and finish up with the compost slightly below the pot rim. The plant should be sitting firmly in the pot, neither too low nor too high, both of which can hinder its growing. Provided the potting is firm, it should be possible to lift the plant by its oldest leaves (not the new growth which could pull out) and the pot will remain. If it falls off the potting was too loose, and you will have to start again! Loose potting will also hinder the plant's progress as it cannot get its roots to cling to the loose material.

Once you are satisfied that the plant is firm and comfortable in its new pot, remember to return the label to the pot and the plant to its growing position. It can be watered in two or three days' time, when any bruising which may have occurred to the roots will have had time to heal.

COMPLETE REPOTTING

Remove the plant from its pot as for 'dropping on'. If squeezing or knocking fails to loosen the plant (cattleyas, for example, are notorious for clinging to the inside of their pots), it may be necessary to cut away the pot. Prepare the plant by removing any surplus pseudobulbs and all dead roots, and trim live roots. All old compost and plant material should be placed in a plastic bag immediately, and not allowed to come into contact with the fresh compost. Old bracts can also be carefully removed.

Select a new or cleaned pot of a size that will allow for a further two years of growth, and try it for size. If at all unsure, opt for a smaller pot. Overpotting means that the plant will be surrounded by too much compost, which will take too long to dry out, and which can therefore lead to loss of the roots: overpotting leads to overwatering, drowning the roots, and possibly killing the plant. It is therefore a mistake to think that an extra-large pot will last the plant a few more years. Underpotting, although the lesser of two evils, will result in the plant having to be repotted again before it should be necessary. Underwatering follows underpotting, and will slow the rate of growth and affecting flowering.

Place crocks in the bottom of the pot and cover with sufficient compost so that the plant will rest with the base of the new growth slightly below the rim of the pot. The roots can be carefully tucked in underneath or, if there is a suitable hollow beneath the plant, fill this with compost before placing in the pot. The oldest (leafless) pseudobulbs can be placed against the pot rim, allowing maximum room at the front for future growth. This applies to the sympodial orchids such as cymbidiums, cattleyas, odontoglossums and all others with pseudobulbs. Paphiopedilums and monopodial orchids (the phalaenopsis, vandas, aerides etc.) can be potted in the same way, but positioned in the centre of the pot. Wherever possible, aerial roots should be left outside the pot, and only buried if it is necessary to hold the plant firm in its pot. Buried aerial roots will suffocate and die. Brittle aerial roots, like those produced by phalaenopsis, can be trimmed back if broken – a broken root will cease to grow from the tip, but will often grow afresh from higher up.

Repotting these orchids requires the same procedure as for dropping on, but more compost may be used as none, or very little, of the old is retained. Be sure to pot firmly (unless using peat), pushing well down with the fingers and adding more compost until the pot is full and the plant firmly held. It should not wobble, or stand too high in the pot. The new growth should be just below the rim of the pot.

REPOTTING INTO BASKETS

Some orchids, particularly *Oncidium flexuosum* and *Maxillaria tenuifolia* produce long plants, their pseudobulbs spreading out along an upward rhizome. This elongated growth produces a plant shape which defies anyone to get it into a conventional pot. For these orchids and many others whose shape decrees some other method of potting, there are wooden baskets made on a square but which can be squeezed into a diamond shape, ideal for long strings of pseudobulbs. The procedure for potting in slatted baskets is the same, but it is useful to line the basket first with something like pea netting to prevent the compost from coming out of the sides. Awkward plants can go from an outgrown pot to a basket very successfully. Initially, plastic-coated wire can be used to wire them in.

ORCHIDS ON BARK

An alternative method is to grow orchids on pieces of bark, fibre poles or tree branches. This is a lovely, natural way to grow many of the species, but is essential that such plants are grown in humid conditions and are kept moist. The plants which will benefit most are those whose shape does not conform to pot culture (brassavolas, epigeneiums etc.) those which like to be grown on the dry side (*Encyclia citrina*) or make most of their roots outside their pot *(Gomeza crispa)*.

Most non-resinous, non-shiny barks are suitable for mounting orchids. Oak or apple branches are ideal. Pieces of Spanish cork bark can be purchased from some orchid nurseries in various sizes, and fibre poles or blocks are also available. Orchids can get their roots into the latter spongy material, and the roots will in no time at all run over the surface of the bark, clinging tightly until they become 'airborne'.

Orchids which are not suitable for bark culture include cymbidiums, *Cattleya* and *Lycaste* type hybrids, all of which would be too large and clumsy and produce heavy root systems more suited to pot culture. Terrestrial orchids, such as paphiopedilums and pleiones would not do well on bark. Phalaenopsis species would be more suitable than hybrids.

If you are taking a plant from a pot on to bark, remove from the pot and prepare it in the same way as for repotting, trimming roots, and removing any surplus pseudobulbs and all old compost.

Have ready the branch, bark or fibre pole you wish to use, plus a length of plastic-coated wire, a pair of pliers, scissors, and a quantity of fresh sphagnum moss, or osmunda fibre. The latter is available, although expensive, from most orchid nurseries. If you are using a piece of cork bark, this should be a little longer than the plant and a wire hook should be placed in the top for hanging. It is now ready for the plant to be mounted.

A small portion of the moss or fibre can be neatly wrapped around the base of the plant, tucking in existing roots, but not covering any of the pseudobulbs. If necessary, add a further portion of moss to the rough side of the bark, at the lower end, and place the plant on this. The moss or fibre base should be larger than the plant, to allow room for it to grow upward and on to the base, and also for roots to enter. To secure the plant and its moss ball to the bark, use plastic-coated wire, passing it between the pseudobulbs and pulling tight. You will find the pliers are the best tool to use for this. Twist the ends of the wire together and cut off any long pieces. The scissors can be used to trim up the base material, to give a nice neat finish. It may be necessary to use two or more wire ties until the plant is firm; a firm hold is just as important as when using a pot. Within six months or so, sufficient new roots should have been made to allow the wire to be removed, and the plant will be self-supporting.

After mounting on the bark, keep the plant sprayed and the moss moist. Give the plant time to adjust to its new type of culture; this could take a season. Some change in the shape of the next pseudobulb may also occur as the different life style affects the plant.

We have stressed that the plants growing on bark are in a much drier habitat than those in a pot. If this presents a problem indoors, it is possible to combine the two types of growing. This is particularly useful where a plant is growing upward out of its pot, each pseudobulb being made higher than the previous one, but at the same time, with a good root system inside the pot. Take the plant from its pot and select another one large enough to contain the plant and either a narrow piece of bark or, better still, a fibre pole. The plant can then be potted up together with the pole securely placed in the pot, leaving the climbing pseudo-bulbs to continue on their way up the pole. When this has been done, the plant can always have a moist base with inside roots, while the rest of it can assume an aerial existence. The best of both worlds! It will often be found where this is done that aerial roots made high up on the plant will run down the pole and into the compost, thereby becoming part aerial and part pot root. Such plants can be sprayed at the top and watered sparingly at the bottom.

Tree branches, mentioned above, can be very successful, and a few mixed orchid species can be included among a variety of the smaller growing bromeliads to great effect. Again owing to the problem of keeping up the humidity around the plants growing on the tree, an indoor growing case is often the best answer.

Plants growing in these semi-natural ways can often be left for a number of years before they need to be disturbed. 'Rebarking' is only required when a plant shown signs of going back, i.e. when the pseudobulbs show a decline in their size. Just sufficient artificial feeds need to be given to keep the foliage a good healthy green.

DIVIDING AND PROPAGATING

Orchids can be grown on for many years to become specimen plants or they can be divided and kept more or less to the same size. This depends upon your needs and the room available. A plant ready for division should be growing in more than one direction and should consist of at least two new growths coming from two separate pseudobulbs or older growths. Provided that at least four pseudobulbs, in leaf and out of leaf, can be retained on each piece, the plant can be split into two or more plants. Four is the minimum number of pseudobulbs with which a plant can be expected to bloom. Making it smaller, therefore, could prevent it from flowering for a year or two while it builds up its strength again.

In addition to the compost and pots have ready a sharp knife or, if you prefer, a pair of secateurs, and some means of sterilizing them. Methylated spirit or a box of matches will do this. Also needed will be a plastic bag for rubbish: old compost, dead roots, and so on.

Remove your plant from its pot and consider the strings of pseudo-bulbs to be kept together and where the division(s) should be. The pseudobulbs are joined by an underground rhizome, (except in *Cattleya* types, where it is clearly visible) and it can be traced by gently prising apart the pseudobulbs. Stand the plant upright, or if easier, lay on its side with the new growths uppermost and slice vertically between the pseudobulbs to sever through the rhizome, which may be quite hard. Careful cutting straight down cannot harm the pseudobulbs, but if the knife slices sideways it will cut into the fleshy base of the pseudobulb and cause 'bleeding' when the sap oozes out. Should this happen, it may be better to remove the damaged pseudobulb, taking care not to repeat the

Dividing and repotting an Oncidium (including root trimming).

An orchid can be divided when it is growing in two or more directions (i.e. new growths on both sides) and when at least three pseudobulbs or growths can be retained by each division. Reducing a plant which is too small can affect its flowering for the next year or two.

The pseudobulbs are joined by a short woody rhizome which can be cut through using a sharp sterilized pruning knife. By counting the pseudobulbs on each division back to the centre, it can be decided where the cut should be made.

All old compost is removed by teasing apart and shaking, leaving the bare roots. Old dead roots (those which come away from the inner core) can be cut off at their base. Very long live roots (white and brittle) can be trimmed back to about 15 cm (6 in).

Each division is potted up separately in a pot which allows room for a further two years' growth. Here the oldest pseudobulb (usually the smallest) can be placed to one side of the pot. More compost will be needed as the root ball was taken apart. Pot firmly!

error with the next. If the pseudobulb is needed to retain the size of the divided plant, or the cut not too severe, dust the damaged portion with sulphur to dry it up and prevent rot from setting in.

Having cut your plant into two, pull the two pieces apart, roots and all. If the root ball is too solid for this, then continue to slice down from between the pseudobulbs, through the compost and roots, as if you were cutting a cake, until you can separate the pieces. It is the same for larger plants; first cut into two, then if desired, into four, and so on.

Once the divisions are laid out, the roots can be trimmed. This is necessary to prevent damaged roots being put back into the pot and rot setting in, Dead roots, identified by their soft outer covering which easily peels away, can be removed altogether, cutting back to their base. Live roots, the plump healthy ones, need to be trimmed to about 15 cm (6 in). These shortened roots will quickly heal over their ends and grow again from higher up. It will be found that anything up to 80 per cent of the root ball may be removed, all of which will be rapidly regained by the plant over the next six months or so. If a plant is found to have no live roots at all, leave some shortened dead ones on for anchorage in the new pot. Sterilize your tools before cutting into another plant.

Check now that your divisions all have more pseudobulbs in leaf than out of leaf. Remove and discard any dead or dying pseudobulbs and leaves. Also remove any other surplus 'back bulbs', as older, leafless pseudobulbs are called, and, if healthy and suitable, pot them on their own as propagations. These propagated pseudobulbs should 'sit' on the compost and not be buried too deeply, which would prevent any new

Developing flower spikes may need some support. Tie them to a bamboo cane to prevent the spike snapping or the plant becoming top heavy. Usually a tie below the lower bud is sufficient.

Orchids growing in a small conservatory. A sizeable collection of plants will be needed to achieve this number in flower at any one time, and to provide a constant, all year round display.

growth from reaching the surface before rotting. If removing more than one leafless pseudobulb, divide and pot up singly, as a group of unseparated pseudobulbs is less likely to produce growths. Very old pseudobulbs may not grow and very small ones are not worth considering. Once potted up, propagated pseudobulbs are kept moist in a warm area until new growth is seen. Grow on in the same way as a seedling (see *Bringing on Young Plants*, below), repotting six months to keep growth steady. At some stage the parent bulb will become exhausted and die, when it can be separated from the new growth which will then become a new, independent plant.

The above applies to most sympodial orchids, but some propagate more easily than others. Cymbidiums will propagate readily from 'back bulbs', but the *Odontoglossum* types will not. Paphiopedilums can only be divided when mature and large enough with several growths.

Dendrobiums of the *nobile* type can also be propagated from the older leafless canes, provided they are not too old and shrivelled. The severed cane can be cut into pieces by cutting between the nodes (where leaves once were) and dipping each end into sulphur or charcoal to dry them up. Fill a pot with compost and place the pieces of cane around the edge with the node on a level with the compost. From some of these nodes, or dormant eyes, will come new growths and roots to form a new plant.

Propagations of this sort will usually commence growth in about six weeks. Until they start to grow they need to be kept just moist. After roots have formed (roots follow top growth), they can be grown on in the same manner as a young plant, with regular 'dropping on' until adult size and flowering which may take up to four years or so.

Monopodial orchids, the phalaenopsis, vandas etc., are not so readily propagated. There is not the surplus growth. Alternative propagating methods can be used but are not easy for the indoor grower and can entail some risk to the plant. Sometimes vandas will, of their own accord, produce young plants from their base. Encourage these and remove from the parent plant when large enough, after about two years.

BRINGING ON YOUNG PLANTS

Raising orchids from seed is not beyond the capabilities of the small indoor grower, although it is a highly specialized field. Anyone interested in raising a new hybrid, or even a species which may be termed rare, would be advised to seek the services of a nursery which is equipped to do the germinating and early growing for you. This work involves the use of a laboratory where the seed is sterilized and sown in sterile flasks on a specially formulated medium which contains the basic nutrients for the germination and growth of the seeds. Anyone with the time and interest could achieve some results at home, but this part of orchid growing would be better left to the experts! It is possible to purchase flasks or bottles of seedlings, which are available from some nurseries and which will contain a small number of plants about one year old. These will be about 1–2 cm ($\frac{1}{2}$–1 in) high, at a stage when they are ready to be taken from the bottle and grown on to flowering, a process which will take another two to three years depending upon the type of orchid.

The best time to remove seedlings is the spring, when they have one growing season ahead of them before the winter. Their first winter is a critical time for them, when losses are likely to occur. Remove the lid or stopper from the bottle and, using tepid water, wash out the seedlings into a bowl and gently clean them of all agar (the medium they were growing in). Have prepared community pots or small seedling trays of moist, fine compost of the type you are using for your adult plants. Any long roots on the seedlings can be trimmed off, they will not serve the seedling in the new compost, and new ones will soon be made, which will be stronger and thicker than those made in the bottle. Ease the seedlings into the compost by making a hole and placing the plant in it, carefully pressing the compost around the plant with the fingers. The seedlings can be planted about 1 cm ($\frac{1}{2}$ in) apart, sitting firmly, but not buried, in the compost. When all the seedlings are potted, the pots or trays can be lightly watered with a rosed can, again using tepid water. Place the seedlings in a warm, shady but not dark area – a case would be ideal – or else under artificial lights. Take care not to overwater, but keep the seedlings just moist. Once new roots start to appear, they can be given a little light feed with every other watering. Check the seedlings every day for signs of damping off. Any which have rotted should be taken out to prevent the rot from spreading. Within six months you should have some fine stocky plants to be proud of. These can be moved on into fresh compost, two or three to a community pot, depending upon their size, in time for the winter. They can be potted up singly the following spring when they will not need to be disturbed again for twelve months. All young life is attractive, and young orchids are no exception. There is a great thrill to watch these babies grow and you will finally be rewarded when you become the first person to see a new hybrid bloom. You may even have the opportunity of choosing a name for it.

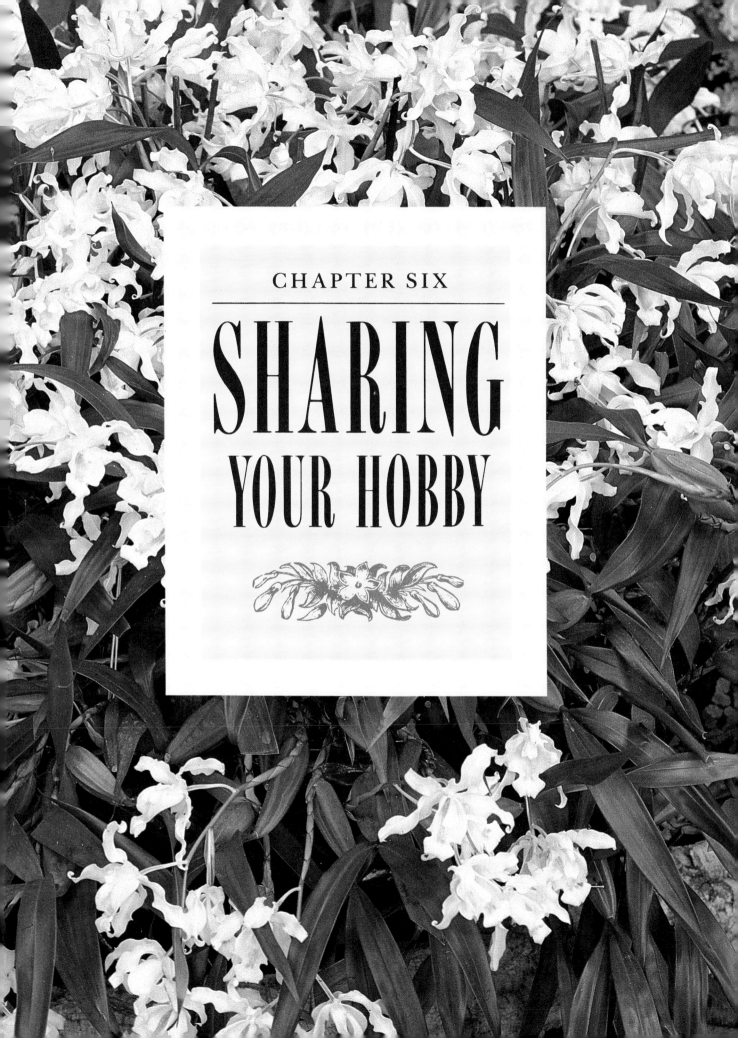

CHAPTER SIX

SHARING
YOUR HOBBY

With interest in orchid growing becoming more widespread throughout the world, enthusiasts everywhere can now receive more encouragement and obtain more help and advice than has previously been possible. There is probably someone living in your vicinity who grows a few and, in this age of motorway travel, your nearest nursery specializing in orchids is possibly only a few hours away. Orchid nurserymen are the experts; when you go to them, whether to buy your first orchids or to seek advice, they want you to return and are only too willing to give you their time and advice freely. These people will sell you the right plants for your conditions when you tell them where you intend growing your orchids. Your first visit to an orchid nursery will undoubtedly amaze you, as you may have been unaware that there are so many kinds of orchids, or that they are so varied. Regular visits to the nursery will reveal to you the whole range of orchids blooming throughout the year. You can also purchase here your orchid compost already mixed for you by the experts,and no doubt a number of other sundry items such as orchid feed and wooden baskets. Most orchid nurseries provide an after-sales service which customers should not be slow to take advantage of. Plants which may be causing concern can be taken along for advice, and often the same nursery will do a repotting service as well, if you do not feel confident enough to do so yourself. In Britain all the major commercial nurseries belong to The British Orchid Growers Association, which publishes a list of its

A group of Cymbidium *hybrids. Plants like these can be summered out-of-doors, and grown and flowered in a conservatory or sun lounge area in the winter.*

members. The secretary's address can be obtained from The Royal Horticultural Society, Vincent Square, London SW1P 2PE.

A few commercial orchid nurseries advertise in the gardening press, where mail order offers are usually a good buy. Again, these nurseries want to keep you as a customer and will only send out good quality plants. The danger here is that if you have ordered from a mail order catalogue you may not be aware of what the orchid or orchids you have chosen should look like, and it may come as a surprise or even a disappointment when you see what you have picked out. Houseplants should look attractive, and it would help to tell the nursery that this is what the orchid is for. If you do not like the look of a purchased plant, the nursery will not mind you telephoning them to query it. What may look to you to be a diseased plant, will probably be quite natural spotting or mottling of the leaves. It is therefore good to have this reassurance from your supplier if you are at all doubtful. Orchid nurserymen are used to this, and they will not mind your queries on what a plant should look like and how best to grow it.

Christmas is a lovely time to give or receive orchids as presents. The most popular types can be seen on sale in many supermarkets, garden centres and florists. The plants in bloom are a much better buy than the cut sprays. The latter may last for eight or ten weeks, but the plant will last a lifetime if well cared for. By all means take advantage of these pot plant orchids, which are generally superbly grown for the home, but bear in mind that the supermarket offers no advice or back-up service. When the plant needs repotting, it is back to the nursery.

ORCHID SOCIETIES

Orchid shows and society meetings are other places where plants are on sale. Here you can see your purchase beforehand, and ask advice at the same time.

In Britain there are about forty amateur orchid societies spread throughout the country. In the USA there are many more, individual societies, the American Orchid Society being the largest in the world. Every major orchid-growing country has its amateur orchid enthusiasts with their own societies. In Britain the majority of the societies come under the umbrella of the British Orchid Council. Members come from all walks of life, and all enjoy the company of others with a shared interest. Societies hold monthly meetings at which a guest speaker is usually invited to lecture. Twice every three years the British Orchid Council hold a congress hosted by one of the societies. These move to a different part of the country each time, with a programme of lectures and a show being the main themes. These congresses have many devotees who regularly attend each one and enjoy the social occasions associated with them.

Your nearest orchid nursery should be able to give you the address of the secretary of the British Orchid Council, from whom you can obtain details of your nearest orchid society. These societies give every encouragement to beginners, and will always help with a problem. Most have table shows at their meetings where members can show their orchids in bloom for the enjoyment of all. By joining an orchid society you have an opportunity of seeing different orchids and making new friends with whom to share your hobby. As more and more are being formed, you may not need to go very far to find one to join.

EXHIBITING

It is not long before pride at having achieved the blooming of a particular orchid leads you to having a go at exhibiting in your local table show. Having seen what others achieve it is always nice to think that your own plant is as good, if not better than, a fellow member's plants. Exhibiting can give a sense of tremendous satisfaction, and if one is lucky enough to be in the ribbons, you may proudly carry home a rosette or two which proclaims to all that you are a successful orchid exhibitor!

Having decided to take the plunge and exhibit your first orchid, study the show catalogue carefully, so that you put it in the right class. If you are not sure, ask the secretary. There is no greater disapppoint-ment than disqualification on a technical point. Some shows have separate classes for orchids grown in a greenhouse and those grown indoors.

Most orchids will need some form of preparation. See that the pot is clean and not water marked, or place it in a suitable pot container. Pseudobulbs should be in a healthy state and cleaned of dead bracts. This not only improves their appearance, but shows that you have no pests hiding beneath. Foliage should be wiped clean, but not polished with leaf shine. The natural look is desired; this may be a dull finish to the leaf and an artificially shiny leaf may lose you points. Any broken leaves or badly marked ones should be removed, provided the plant can spare them. Black tips can be trimmed for neatness.

Finally, the flowers. A plant is at its best for exhibiting when all, or the majority of, its blooms are fully open. If less than half its blooms are open, the plant is hardly suitable for exhibiting. If the blooms have been out a long time and show signs of old age, the judges will not look upon it favourably either. Tall flower spikes will require some staking for support, as well as additional supporting canes while they are being transported to a show, which can be removed at the show. While some species need little or no support for their flowers, others will be found to need special techniques for their blooms to be shown off to their best advantage.

Cymbidiums, odontoglossums, phalaenopsis and other orchids which produce long flower spikes will need a supporting bamboo cane to hold the spike. The cane should be just thick enough to support without looking obtrusive. Split green canes are suitable for all but the heaviest of spikes. The cane should be inserted vertically into the compost, as close as possible to the spike and away from the rim of the pot where most of the roots are. The cane needs to be just shorter than the spike. The flower spike is then brought close to the cane and tied to it. The fewer number of ties the better, often one or two are all that are needed. Twisted or bent spikes may need a few more ties in an effort to straighten them out, but be careful, they are easily snapped. The way to avoid this problem is to train the spike from an early stage, using a loose tie which can be slid upward as the flower spike extends. A naturally arching habit is to be preferred over an upright one, and this is easily achieved by leaving the buds to arch from an early stage.

Trying to tie up a spike whose flowers have opened on a horizontal stem will result in the blooms being shown on their side, or upside down, and they will not right themselves once they have opened fully. More lost points!

Dendrobiums may need their canes supporting in a similar way, while the flowers, being on very short stems, remain untied.

Paphiopedilums need not have their bloom stem tied up unless the weight of the bud is pulling it down. After the flower has opened and become set – within a few days – it can be brought upright and supported by a short cane cut off behind the dorsal (top) petal. One tie

Exhibiting your orchids at shows and competing for rosettes can be a very satisfying aspect of your hobby. Amateur orchid shows encourage a good standard of culture and are a lot of fun.

immediately behind the flower and another about halfway along the stem is all that will be required to place the flower at exactly the right angle so that it can be looked fully in the face and does not hang down.

Cattleyas and their types are variable. Those whose blooms open looking well forward without drooping will not need supporting, except for travelling. Those whose blooms hang down, or arc so close they are touching, or preventing each other from opening fully, need a different type of staking. Using one thin green split bamboo cane for each bloom, cut each one just short of the tip of the dorsal petal while the bloom is being held in the desired position. Make a split 5 cm (2 in) long in the top of each cane and insert in the pot. With careful manipulation place the stem in the split, so that the cane holds it in position from immediately behind the bloom. With a little practice it will be found that you can easily adjust the canes and twist them round until all the flowers are facing the right way and the right distance apart. Lycastes can be treated in a similar way.

Canes placed at an angle look untidy and may be top heavy. It is always better for the canes to be upright and the spikes brought to them.

Most of the smaller type of species will need no support for their flowers at all and they can be exhibited as they are, their own natural habit showing off the blooms to their best advantage.

Any orchid plant is worthy of being placed on a show bench provided it is a healthy mature plant (or a young plant in a special class for first-time flowers) which is clean and free from pests and disease. If pests are found or a virus disease suspected the exhibitor may be asked to remove the plant immediately. The plant should also be flowering to the best of its ability at the time of the show. On the bench you can compare your plant with others in the same class. You may feel very satisfied with your own plant, or realize how you could improve it for another year.

The judges will be taking into account the size and health of your plant as well as the number and quality of the flowers. The latter entails the texture, shape and colouring of the blooms.

From small table exhibits, it is possible to progress to the bigger shows organized by other societies in your area, or to which you are willing to travel. Your society may be one of those which stages a collective exhibit at one of the major exhibitions organized by an orchid association. In this way you can see your orchids doing their bit to provide a really good exhibit open to the public. Other major shows encourage individual entries with numerous classes to suit every orchid plant. By studying the judges' decisions you can begin to learn what they are looking for and which plants are getting the highest points and ribbons.

AWARDS

Having gained experience at exhibiting your orchids, the highest accolade you can achieve in Britain is a coveted award or certificate from the Royal Horticultural Society. A specially selected orchid committee meet in London and occasionally elsewhere once a month to consider for awards any plant which is submitted to them. Only the very best orchids are displayed, and entries come from all over the world, particularly for the meeting at the world-famous Chelsea Flower Show. While the First Class Certificate (FCC/RHS) and Award of Merit (AM/RHS) are extremely difficult, but not impossible, for an indoor grower to achieve, their Certificate of Cultural Commendation

Opposite: A group of Paphiopedilum *hybrids, showing a good selection of these warm growing, low light plants. Very long lasting during the winter months.*

(CCC/RHS) is within the reach of the grower of a particularly fine and well-grown specimen. To be worthy of a CCC/RHS the grower must submit a plant which has been grown on into a specimen size (a process which can take many years) and is considered exceptional by the committee. It must be in full bloom when exhibited and should reflect a consistently high standard of culture. Before submitting a plant to the RHS for any of their awards, you would be advised to talk to your nearest professional grower, who will know whether it would be worth the time and trouble involved. In the USA awards of an equally high standard can be gained from the American Orchid Society.

Apart from exhibiting individual select plants to the RHS orchid committee, a group of orchids can be staged at any one of their shows to gain an RHS medal. A very few amateur growers indeed reach these heights, but this is the ultimate to which a grower may succeed, but not without a great deal of hard work and dedication, and a huge collection of orchids from which to draw the very best.

JUDGING

Although an RHS Gold Medal may be beyond most growers, for those who are nevertheless successful exhibitors, or are simply interested in the finer points of showing and wish to become more involved, it is possible to become a qualified orchid judge. The British Orchid Council organize regular judging seminars throughout the country to encourage and train their own judges. Your local orchid society secretary will have information on this. A similar system for producing judges is organized by the American Orchid Society, and other systems exist in the major orchid-growing countries.

PUBLICATIONS AND CONFERENCES

Many amateur growers aspire to writing about their own experiences with orchids, articles from which everyone can learn. While the general gardening press carries the occasional article on orchids, if you have exhausted the many books which are now available on the subject, you may find additional enjoyable reading in the specialized orchid journals. In all the major orchid-growing countries there is at least one magazine devoted entirely to orchids, and information about it should be available from your local society secretary. These magazines are not normally sold through newsagents because of their specialized nature. In Britain the *Orchid Review* – write to the Royal Horticultural Society, Vincent Square, London SW1P 2PE for this – is the oldest orchid publication, having been in print without a break since 1893. It caters for everyone interested in orchids, whether novice window-sill grower or experienced nurseryman. From it you can find out all that is happening in the orchid world, from your forthcoming society show to the next world orchid conference, held every third year in a different country. They have become popular social gatherings where you can listen to lectures on all aspects of orchids.

So it can be seen that the opportunities for the orchid enthusiast are endless, you can indulge your hobby to any lengths you care to go to. Many do, and find that orchid growing goes hand in hand with spontaneous friendship across the world.

CHAPTER SEVEN

MONTHLY CALENDAR NOTES

*T*hese monthly notes are intended to make the grower aware of the different stages at which his orchids should be at any time of the year and how to treat them. Whether it is a dropped yellow leaf or the start of new growth, we have tried to give the reader some idea what to expect from their orchids and when. These notes are meant as helpful guidelines – some orchids may not always conform exactly.

JANUARY
(NORTHERN HEMISPHERE)
JULY
(SOUTHERN HEMISPHERE)

FLOWERS

This is one of the quietest months for orchids, with many of them at rest. It is also one of the most colourful, as a lot of the most popular kinds are in bloom. Those excellent and showy Christmas gifts – the cymbidiums – should be in their prime, with several weeks of blooming still left. Check that all young flowers spikes are well supported. During their flowering season they can be placed in the best position to show off their blooms, a central table display perhaps, or on a sideboard. Provided they are away from any source of heat, such as a radiator or television set, they may remain on show until the flowers are over before being found a suitable growing place. Some may already have new growths showing, which will grow better when the flowers are removed.

RESTING

Take a look at those orchids which are resting, which will include the coelogynes, dendrobiums, encyclias and lycastes. Check that pseudobulbs or canes are plump. If some shrivelling of the oldest pseudobulbs is occurring leave the plant dry, but if the newest pseudobulb is also shrivelling, some water should be given. One moderate application of water should be enough to wet the compost throughout, and the pseudobulbs will gradually plump up again. Midwinter shrivelling of leading pseudobulbs is usually caused by underwatering the previous summer, or cutting down the watering too early towards the end of the growing season. How long it will take for the leading pseudobulbs to plump up depends upon the state of the roots, and whether they too are completely dormant or not at this time.

WATERING

Those orchids which have continued to grow during the winter can be kept just moist. These include the hybrid cymbidiums, *Odontoglossum* types, paphiopedilums as well as phalaenopsis and others, all of which will have new growths or leaves developing, albeit at a slow rate. To retain some moisture will take far less water than in the summer, so care should be taken not to overwater at this time, and no harm will come to plants allowed to dry out between waterings.

FEEDING

The growth of orchids will naturally slow down in time with the shorter days and lack of light. Unless the plants are growing under totally artificial lights, it is extremely difficult to get enough light to them to warrant giving any additional food. While opinions vary on this point, we have always preferred to give the plants a rest from feeding, which in our opinion they do not require at this time of year, as it can result in a build-up of unused chemicals in the compost, which in turn will cause problems when new roots commence.

HUMIDITY AND ROTS

One problem which can arise from the slowing of growth and short, dull days is rot. Take extra care with the humidity trays, allowing them to dry out for a time. Too much humidity at a time when the light is poor and there is little fluctuation in temperature can create good conditions for moulds to grow and rots to start. Any sign of rot around the base of a plant on the pseudobulbs should be treated immediately. Old pseudo-bulbs can also start to die naturally at this time, turning yellow or brown and becoming soft. Remove when you see they are dying.

TEMPERATURE

Temperatures should not be too high at night for the cool-growing orchids: aim at 10°C (50°F) as the ideal. Any warmer than this can produce a softer growth which will not flower, but a drop of 4–9°C (10–15°F) will stop all growth and make it difficult for some of them to commence growing again at the right time. Fluctuation in temperature is also necessary, so a rise of 7 or 9°C (10 or 15°F) during the day will greatly assist their growing.

By the end of this month, it should be possible to see new growths coming on some of the species. Unless they have been kept too dark, they will be responding to the gradually lengthening days.

FEBRUARY
(NORTHERN HEMISPHERE)
AUGUST
(SOUTHERN HEMISPHERE)

WATERING

Those among the species which are just starting their new growth may now be watered sparingly. When these have grown to about 5 cm (2 in) high, the new roots will commence, and from this time on normal watering may be resumed. It is during this and the coming months that most attention should be paid to watering; plants with fast-developing growth should not be allowed to dry out. All except the soft-leaved lycastes can be regularly sprayed. A new growth subjected to dryness in the air or in the pot can slow its growth dramatically, causing corrugation of the leaves, only apparent at a later stage. In the case of *Coelogyne ochracea*, where the encircling young leaves are curled tightly, they can become sticky with a sugary substance secreted by the plant. If not washed off by regular spraying, it will stick the young leaves together, which retards their development and causes problems for the flower buds pushing up through the centre of the young growth. If their progress is impeded, the flower spike will not develop.

BUDS

The earliest of the dendrobiums to bloom, species such as *D. wardianum* and *D. aureum*, will be coming into bud now. Look for the green nodes swelling on the leafless canes. These will gradually produce buds at the same time as the new growth starts at the base. *D. nobile* should not be watered until the buds are clearly visible, otherwise moisture encourages these embryo buds to produce leaves instead, becoming adventitious growths at the expense of flowers.

FEEDING

Towards the end of this month give one nitrate-based feed to all the orchids which are now visibly growing. By now it is possible to get sudden bursts of sunshine. Already the sun is gaining in power, and at midday could be strong enough to cause burn marks on the more tender leaves which are exposed to it. The orchids have not been used to such brightness and after the dull winter it is as well to introduce them gradually to the extra light. The drawing of net curtains to protect those growing close to a window sill will be sufficient. A slight change of colour in the foliage of the *Odontoglossum* types is all to the good, provided it is slight. This reddish 'tan' will continue to intensify during the spring months. Flowers also should be kept out of the sun otherwise premature spotting and fading may occur.

TEMPERATURE

As the light improves and hopefully a little more occasional sunshine is seen, so daytime temperatures will start to rise. This is all to the good of the orchids, causing a greater fluctuation than has been possible since the start of the winter, although there should be no fear of them getting too warm. At night the air will still be dropping to 10°C (50°F). The aim should be cool at night, warm by day.

REPOTTING

It is not too early to consider the spring potting which, if each plant is done at the right time to suit it, will last into the early summer. Those plants which have already finished flowering and whose new growths are visible can be done without further delay. If the new growths have not yet started, delay repotting until they are seen. Those orchids whose flowers are produced from the new growth, mainly pleiones and some coelogynes, can either be repotted before or after flowering. If left until after flowering it will be found that their new roots have already started, and these could be damaged in the process. If you repot before flowering, do so early so as not to cause the fast-growing buds to abort.

FLOWER SPIKES

All the spring-flowering orchids will be showing their flower spikes now. Take care with supporting canes and use only as necessary, where there is a danger of long or heavy spikes snapping under their own weight, or being accidentally caught by the watering can. Flowering paphiopedilums should be making a good show now. On the spring-flowering cattleyas, buds may already be visible at the base of the sheath. Some hybrids produce a double sheath, making it impossible to see the buds inside the second one. To ensure the developing buds can emerge safely, cut the top of the outside sheath and split the sides to allow some air to the inside sheath. A few greenfly could find their way on to the buds: watch out for this annoying pest, and remove with a small artist's brush or rinse the buds under the tap or in a bowl of water.

Odontoglossum types are among those orchids which could be showing flower spikes at this time; it is always exciting to find them just showing inside the first leaf on the latest pseudobulb. If, however, instead of a flower spike a new growth is started, this means that, alas, the plant will not bloom this year, or any year, from that pseudobulb. Maybe the plant had been kept too warm at night, or did not get enough light when the pseudobulb was making up. Another year, the pseudobulb will be making up at a different time, and the problem will solve itself.

MARCH
(NORTHERN HEMISPHERE)
SEPTEMBER
(SOUTHERN HEMISPHERE)

ORCHID SHOWS

This is probably the most rewarding month of the year for orchid growers, in more ways than one. Being the height of the main flowering season we can enjoy the majority of orchids in bloom in our own collection, and also visit some of the many orchid exhibitions being held at this time. It is always worth seeing other orchids in bloom, and these shows provide a chance to gain more knowledge from the experts and enjoy new varieties not previously seen. This is also the best way to purchase any new additions to your collection. Having found the plant of your choice you can enquire whether it is suitable for your conditions, when it will need repotting etc. Professional people never tire of giving such advice. To find out details of these shows get in touch with an orchid society or The Royal Horticultural Society (see page 112).

REPOTTING

Most of the repotting will be done this month. As the plants' growth rate increases, they will take very little time to settle down again in their new compost, and before long those very rewarding new roots will be seen exploring their new territory. Orchids in flower spike may need to be left until the autumn.

WATERING

From now on watering and feeding can be increased, keeping all growing plants in an evenly moist condition. Light spraying or daily sponging of the leaves will keep the foliage fresh. The exceptions to spraying are the soft-leaved *Lycaste* types, and pleiones. The paphiopedilums may be sprayed very lightly, just enough to lay a 'dew' on the leaves without it running down to collect in the growths. Water accumulating here can all too easily cause a rot to commence. In their wild state, surplus water would be dried up very quickly by the sun and wind. In a greenhouse it will dry up quicker than indoors because of the more even temperature, so extra care should be taken indoors.

PESTS

Spring is the time for rebirth, and this applies to garden pests as well! Somehow some insect pests and mites find their way indoors on to our beloved plants, and soon, as the weather turns milder, they will make their presence felt. Watch out for the various types of scale insects, mealy bug and red spider mites. Small slugs and snails might also be present, the eggs perhaps brought indoors, in the compost.

TEMPERATURE

This should be kept about the same for the cool house orchids, perhaps running a little higher during the days when the sun shines. The warmer-growing phalaenopsis and others growing in an indoor case will be able to have more air if the glass front can be left open now during the day. At night the case should be maintained at a temperature as close to 18°C (65°F) as possible. Phalaenopsis will not die if grown cooler, but neither will they be at their best.

LIGHT AND FEEDING

Keep the growing orchids in good light, but beware of bright spring sunshine on the young leaves. It may be necessary to move plants which are standing in a window into the room a bit more to avoid direct sunlight. If they cannot be easily moved, place net curtaining between the plants and the window. On bright days, also check that the daytime temperature is not rising higher than say 24–27°C (75–80°F) in a window area. With central heating still on in the house, it is surprising how warm it can get in an alcove when the sun is shining. If the plants are having early morning or late afternoon and evening sun, which will not be too harmful for them, keep the foliage dry while the sun is there, and spray as soon as the sun has passed over the plants. Keep all flowers away from the continual glare of direct sunlight, as it will tone down the colours and cause premature spotting. It can also harm softer buds, which will be more easily burnt than the foliage. Foliage which may have become dark green through lack of light in the winter, should now be changing slightly, turning from mid to light green. depending upon the type, to indicate more light being received. Give two feeds during this month.

APRIL
(N O R T H E R N   H E M I S P H E R E)
O C T O B E R
(S O U T H E R N   H E M I S P H E R E)

TEMPERATURE

Temperatures should be running a few degrees higher now: for the cool-growing orchids between 10 and 13°C (50–55°F) at night and anything from a 7°C (10°F) to 14°C (20°F) lift during the day. The warmer-growing varieties should be 7°C (10°F) higher for much of the time.

FEEDING AND WATERING

Higher temperatures and longer daylight hours will be reflected in the growth of the plants, and the feeding programme can be stepped up as a result. From the beginning of this month feed the orchids about every ten days, using the same basic weak feed, and giving at least one watering in between. The feeding should correct the foliage colour and prevent it from becoming too light or yellowish.

REPOTTING

The last of the resting orchids should be starting into new growth now and they can be repotted if necessary. By the end of this month most of the repotting should be completed, leaving only those plants which are flowering at this time.

PESTS

Plants which have been repotted for a month or two can sometimes get a visitation from springtails, the eggs having arrived in the compost. These minute insects can be seen usually only when a pot is lifted and they are to be found clustered beneath. Look out for woodlice in the same places and destroy with a little Jeyes fluid sprayed over the area when they are seen. This is a good month to spend some time wiping the leaves of all the orchids, where this is possible, as a precaution against red spider mite. This is one pest which can actually be worse indoors than in a greenhouse as the drier atmosphere suits it well. Other pests to look out for at the same time are scale insects and mealy bugs.

FLOWERS

The cymbidiums' flowering season will be coming to an end, with just a few of the later blooming varieties still in bud or flower to last a few more weeks. The *Odontoglossum* types will be demonstrating their huge variety, with all other colours and shapes possible. The long-stemmed types will need supporting, but it is up to the grower whether to leave the spike with an arching habit or to train upright with ties. The cattleyas, growing where there is sufficient room and light for them, will also be blooming about this time. Those buds out of their sheaths can have supporting canes to show off the blooms better, and at the same time to prevent them from snapping off – some of the heavier heads of flowers can break under their own weight. Many of the summer-flowering miltoniopsis will be showing their flower spikes now, from half-mature new growths or newly completed pseudobulbs.

MAY
(NORTHERN HEMISPHERE)
NOVEMBER
(SOUTHERN HEMISPHERE)

This is the month when visitors from all over the world flock to the famous Chelsea Flower Show in London. Organized by The Royal Horticultural Society, this is the largest annual flower show in the world. Every type of plant imaginable is on display, and every fancier can find their particular field well represented. So it is true of the orchids and every year large exhibits from amateur and commercial growers endeavour to show the many facets of orchids to would-be enthusiasts as well as experienced hobbyists. A visit to such a show is always well worth while, so much can be learned from chatting with other growers.

LIGHT

The new growth on the orchids progresses at a rapid pace, and the feeding and watering continues at the same rate. Protect the new growths from too much light by facing them away from the window.

Those orchids which enjoy the shadiest conditions may need to be moved now if they have been in a lighter growing spot during the winter and spring. These include paphiopedilums and phalaenopsis other than those being grown in an indoor case. If they are now getting too much light it will show in the leaves of paphiopedilums by turning them yellowish, with possibly some die-back from the tips. The phalaenopsis also will lose their good green colour, the leaves becoming yellowish, or showing pitted yellowing patches, the latter caused by the collapse of leaf cells on the fleshy foliage. While these and other orchids require protection from the sustained glare of the sun, they should not be deprived of light, and too little light resulting from being placed in a dark corner or similar dimly lit area will not produce good growth. Very young seedlings should also be treated with care and placed alongside the shade-seeking paphiopedilums until they are a few years old.

WATERING

All plants should by now be over their resting periods and being watered normally, always trying to achieve an evenly moist state of the compost. Those plants receiving the most light will naturally be drying out at a faster rate than those in the confines of the indoor case. It will also be noticed that when spraying, the foliage of those plants standing directly in the window will dry out faster.

HUMIDITY TRAYS

Higher temperatures, increased feeding, longer days, all these factors will combine to encourage the unwanted growth of algae, mosses or moulds which may appear in or surrounding the humidity trays, or on the surface of the pots. Remove this foreign greenery from the orchids, as it will clog up the surface compost and create a problem when watering. The only permissible moss, which grows so well with orchids, is sphagnum moss. Where this is used in the compost, its surface growth enhances the pot and gives the grower a guide to watering by turning grey when the compost requires watering. Other growing matter should be discouraged. Any stale or green water in the humidity trays should be tipped out, the base pebbles washed through a seive and replaced with clean water on top. A few drops of Jeyes fluid in the water should keep the tray clean. The indoor growing case may have moulds growing on the inside which can be wiped clean, again using a little Jeyes fluid to control its growth.

Shortly after repotting, if using a bark compost, small toadstools are likely to appear on the surface. While these are harmless enough, and merely reflect the organic nature of the compost, they are best pulled out and not left to decay on the surface.

JUNE
(NORTHERN HEMISPHERE)
DECEMBER
(SOUTHERN HEMISPHERE)

This month sees the longest days and the plants continue to grow apace. Many will be nearing completion of their pseudobulbs. Now it can be determined if they are of good size, hopefully if all has gone well, quite a bit larger than in previous years. As the pseudobulbs swell to maturity, those plants can be turned so that the newly grown pseudobulbs face the light to ensure ripening which in turn will lead to flowering. The newly completed pseudobulbs on the *Odontoglossum* types will show their flower spikes any time now, indicating blooms for late summer and onwards.

PESTS

Greenfly are quite likely to appear on flower buds as well as new growths. These are mostly easily seen and easily controlled (see page 86). Red spider mite is not so easy to see yet is far more harmful. Watch out for it on the undersides of the leaves, in particular the youngest leaves.

REPOTTING

This is the very latest opportunity for repotting plants which may only just have finished flowering. If possible 'drop on' without causing undue disturbance to the plant. If the repotting is not urgent, it may be better to leave the plant until a more suitable time, possibly the autumn. Plants repotted earlier should be making plenty of new roots now; in particular any aerial roots appearing outside the pots or from plants growing in baskets should be encouraged. Take care not to damage them, and spray lightly and as often as possible, up to three times a day in warm sunny weather.

SUMMERING OUT-OF-DOORS

Towards the end of this month is about the right time to put those plants which are suitable out of doors for the summer. These plants should be established in their pots with a sturdy root system. Any newly repotted plants, or sickly plants may suffer from shock resulting from the dramatically different outdoor conditions, and these would be better left where they are. Only large, healthy plants will benefit from summering outdoors, the main aim being to produce a harder growth which will bloom more freely. For this reason those plants which are reluctant to bloom, but which are healthy enough to do so, will respond best. Prepare a suitable position for your plants, ideally placing them on a bench against a wall or fence where they will get the early morning or late evening but not the midday sun. It is best to start with a few selected plants to see how they cope, watching carefully for signs of stress, such as too much loss of foliage, or yellowing of leaves. While some is to be expected, as the plants come to terms with their changed environment, this should not cause the plants to suffer, and after the initial settling down period of about two weeks, they should be seen to improve their growth dramatically. The change in temperature should not be all that great, as the days get warmer and the conservatory temperature rises, it will remain about the same out-of-doors. Care should be taken with watering outside during bright sunny spells: more water will be needed, as strong winds will also cause them to dry out, while days of heavy rain may mean some covering will be needed to prevent saturation, although they will obviously dry out much faster than indoors. Be wary of placing out of doors the shade-loving orchids, those growing in an indoor case, and also very young seedlings which would not be able to cope. Also leave inside plants about to bloom.

JULY
(NORTHERN HEMISPHERE)
JANUARY
(SOUTHERN HEMISPHERE)

TEMPERATURE

The orchids left inside may be coping with temperatures at their maximum during the day. Growing cases and rooms are not liable to overheat, but sun lounges and conservatories may. Ideally, the daytime temperature should not exceed 30°C (86°F) during the day, and this can usually be controlled by blinds, damping down where possible to increase the humidity, and by keeping doors and windows open. A breeze blowing through the plants is all to the good, and should not be mistaken for a cold draught. The orchids will cope with these high temperatures during the day provided there is plenty of moisture around their roots and a cooling down at night – a drop to 13–16°C (55–61°F) will allow sufficient fluctuation. If temperatures are remaining to high or too constant, the plants would do better out of doors. Heat without light is to be avoided. An ill-lit back room, for example, where a solitary plant is left with insufficient light, but in a constantly warm and stuffy atmosphere, is not a place to produce good growth. Again, better to place the plant out of doors from now on.

FEEDING

Plants coping with extra light may be given a little extra feed. Use a slightly stronger dosage every ten days or so. By the end of the month change to a phosphate-based feed for those plants which have completed their season's pseudobulbs or new growths. This will be a further aid in encouraging blooms.

Check that all pseudobulbs, newly completed and older ones, are fully plump. Pseudobulbs shrivelling in the summer through lack of water create trouble later in the year.

FLOWERING

The summer-flowering orchids, many of which are beautifully fragrant, will be blooming now, in particular the miltoniopsis in shades of white and pastel pink through to the rich reds, the encyclias and a few maxillarias. Phalaenopsis blooms, which come at all times of the year, will last longer if kept out of the sun as this can cause blooms to wilt prematurely and burn marks or early spotting can occur. Bright light can also affect colours, particularly on the odontoglossums: it may fade the bright colours, especially the yellows, and cause pink tones on the white blooms. Usually, it is the buds which are affected, showing on the outside of the sepals on opened blooms. This is not considered in any way harmful, but can explain why a white-flowered *Odontoglossum* will apparently change its colour when blooming at a different time of the year.

GROWTH

Do not disturb orchids at this time of the year while they are having to cope with high temperatures. Many of them will begin to slow their growth now, although not so dramatically as in the winter. Those orchids which bloom from the newly completed pseudobulb will be slowing down in preparation for their flowering.

AUGUST
(NORTHERN HEMISPHERE)
FEBRUARY
(SOUTHERN HEMISPHERE)

LIGHT

This is a good time of the year to check that the foliage on your orchids remains a good shade of green. If too much light has been getting to them, or if they have been fed too little or not at all, they may by now be turning from a healthy green to a yellow green. This could also be the case if a particular plant has not been repotted for a few years and has used up all the nourishment available in the compost. This yellowing of foliage also applies to plants being grown out of doors for the summer. The problem is not a great one, but it is a warning that plants may be reaching the limit of their light endurance and any more would cause distress in the form of premature leaf loss, or leaves browning from the tips. The situation may be improved by moving the plants to a shadier spot and if necessary increasing the feed slightly.

FLOWER SPIKES

Many pseudobulbs will be making up now, their seasonal growth almost complete. The feed can be changed to a phosphate-based one to encourage flowering. Cymbidiums will already be coming into flower spike, always an exciting climax to months of growing. The flower spikes appear from the base of the last completed pseudobulb, either on the outside or inside the first leaf. They are round and plump, the shape and size of a pencil, sometimes dark in colour. They vary from the flatter, greener new growth which very soon fans out into new leaves. The flower spike continues to extend, often growing out at an angle which needs to be straightened by tying loosely to a supporting bamboo cane. Insert the cane close to the flower and spike, away from the rim of the pot where most roots are to be found. As the spike continues to grow so extra ties can support it. This will not only keep the spike upright, it will also prevent snapping which can occur on heavy spikes. Do not tie between the buds – the flowers will look at their best if the buds are left to arch naturally.

WINTER CARE

Those orchids which do not have much of a resting period, the *Odontoglossum* types, some cattleyas, cymbidiums and phalaenopsis in particular, will often produce new growths or a leaf now, which means they will need to be watered throughout the coming winter. Coelogynes, maxillarias, lycastes, dendrobiums and many others will be completing their pseudobulbs. Continue to water these plants, keeping them moist all the time to ensure their pseudobulbs are developing as large as possible.

SEPTEMBER
(NORTHERN HEMISPHERE)
MARCH
(SOUTHERN HEMISPHERE)

REPOTTING

Those orchids which will be growing throughout the winter will be showing new growth by now, and this is therefore a good time to repot. Second to the spring months, this is the best time to move plants on, now that the worst of the summer heat is over. The plants will have six weeks or so to settle down and establish new roots before their growth slows down considerably as the winter advances. The *Odontoglossum* type hybrids, miltoniopsis, *Cattleya* type hybrids, paphiopedilums and phalaenopsis are among those orchids which will benefit most from repotting now, provided they are showing new growth, or are about to do so. Any which are in flower spike should not be disturbed, and would be better left until the spring, after they have flowered. Repotting a plant in bud or flower spike can hinder the development of buds, or cause advanced buds to turn yellow and drop off.

Wherever possible, repotting at this time should be confined to 'dropping on'. This is very useful where the existing compost is in good condition and is of the same mix as you are using. It minimizes the disturbance to the plant and is particularly beneficial for moving on young seedlings or propagations which need a slightly larger pot every six months or so.

GROWING OUTSIDE

Towards the end of this month, those plants which have spent the summer out-of-doors, should come in. Night temperatures will soon be dropping well below 10°C (50°F) which could check the growth. If they have progressed well and produced firm pseudobulbs many will be found to be in flower spike. Check the plants over for insect pests, woodlice, springtails and weevils. A few slug pellets will take care of slugs and small snails. Alternatively, place a few apple slices on the surface of the compost: leave overnight, then turn the apple over to discover the slugs and perhaps woodlice and springtails, underneath. Otherwise a watering with a weak solution of Jeyes fluid will clear them out. Check also the surface of the compost. If a carpet of moss has grown, remove it. If the surface looks discoloured with moulds or scum remove this also and resurface the plants with fresh compost. Trim or remove any damaged leaves and finally clean each leaf with a leaf wipe to remove dirt and any pests such as red spider mite, mealy bug and scale insects. Remove any old bracts on the cymbidiums; pests can live among them and remain undetected. Your plants should now be clean and tidy and ready to return to their winter quarters.

OCTOBER
(NORTHERN HEMISPHERE)
APRIL
(SOUTHERN HEMISPHERE)

TEMPERATURE AND LIGHT

As the temperature begins to get lower at night as well as by day, so extra light can be given to the orchids. Conservatory-grown plants can now cope with all the light they can get, so any shade in use during the summer can now be taken down to allow maximum light to reach the plants. Indoors, conditions are more stable and there is little or nothing extra required. Light now is more important, and on bright days the plants will benefit. Unless grown under artificial light, from now on they will receive little light of sufficient strength to be of much value.

FEEDING

Towards the end of this month the feeding can be gradually lessened, while watering remains the same. Paphiopedilums, phalaenopsis and others which are growing in a warmer area and which will continue to grow throughout the winter can be kept fed throughout. The strength of the feed can be slightly reduced to allow for the slower growth being made. The same orchids growing in a completely controlled environment, such as a growing case or room where artificial lighting is used, can continue to be fed at the same rate as in the summer, merely changing from a nitrate-based food to a phosphate-based one. Their continuous growth will ensure the feed is taken up by the plants.

RESTING

Between now and the end of the year the deciduous orchids such as pleiones, some dendrobiums and lycastes will shed their leaves. At the first signs of yellowing and spotting the watering can stop. When the leaves finally drop the plants may need to be moved to winter quarters. Ideally they will need a cool (10°C, 50°F), light place where they can be left dry until the spring. The evergreen resting orchids, which include coelogynes, encyclias and maxillarias among others will lose one or two leaves from the oldest pseudobulbs only. Feeding can be stopped and watering can be gradually reduced over the next four to six weeks. Pseudobulbs which look as if they have finished growing may still be swelling, if watering is stopped too soon before they have absorbed their maximum, shrivelling during the winter will result. Those orchids which are showing aerial roots can be checked to see whether these roots are becoming dormant. When the green growing tip becomes covered by the velamen the root will not be active. This will occur with phalaenopsis, vandas etc., and indicates that the plant is resting. However, these monopdial orchids should not be kept dry for too long, and a 'semi-dry' rest is called for. This means giving just sufficient water to prevent dehydration of the leaves. Alternatively, lightly spraying the leaves while leaving the compost dry is a good solution. Pleiones need only a light dry and frost-free place to winter in. The unheated spare bedroom window sill will probably suit very well.

NOVEMBER
(NORTHERN HEMISPHERE)
MAY
(SOUTHERN HEMISPHERE)

FLOWERING

From now on until the spring there is little to do to the orchids except enjoy their long-lasting blooms. Cymbidiums will have begun to bloom now, while the cattleyas will be well into their season. The winter-blooming paphiopedilums will be in advanced bud ready for a show later on, and many other orchids will be blooming soon. Keep a constant check for greenfly on the buds and remove by washing off.

TEMPERATURE

For the cool house orchids temperatures should not drop below 10°C (50°F) at night. By now the heating should be on at night to maintain this minimum which should rise during the day by at least 5°C (10°F) and more if the sun reaches the plants. The warmer-growing orchids will need to be provided with a more constant temperature as their night-time requirements are nearer to 18°C (64°F). Again a daytime rise of several degrees is advisable. Cool orchids growing too warm, particularly at night, and warm orchids being too cold can both upset the growth pattern of the plants and cause flower spikes to wilt and buds to abort.

WATERING

The watering of the orchids will be at a minimum now. Just sufficient water will be needed by the continuously growing orchids, i.e. cymbidiums, *Odontoglossum* types, paphiopedilums and phalaenopsis, to keep them moist. This will mean watering far less often as the plants take longer to dry out.

BUYING PLANTS AND FLOWERS

At this time of year orchids become available both as pot plants and cut blooms in florists and stores. Both make super gifts and the plants usually present exceptionally good value. The purchaser can select plants in flower with some buds yet to come, knowing the blooms are fresh and will remain in their prime for about eight weeks. Once a cymbidium flower ages, the first sign is a reddening of the lip which indicates the end of its life. This should be borne in mind when selecting a plant, even more so if your choice is a single boxed bloom. The flower expected to last eight weeks may already be seven weeks old!

DECEMBER
(NORTHERN HEMISPHERE)
JUNE
(SOUTHERN HEMISPHERE)

RESTING

Another quiet month for the orchids, many of which will have been dormant for some time. Check these resting orchids, both deciduous and evergreen types, for any kind of damp marks or rots. These may appear in the crowns of the monopodial orchids and also the paphiopedilums, and it is as well to be on the lookout for the first signs of trouble. Crown rots are usually the result of water being retained in the axil of the leaves where the tender new leaf is yet to come. It happens particularly at this time of the year when temperatures are at their lowest and growth is slow. The growing centres of phalaenopsis and vandas can be treated with sulphur to prevent the rot spreading and the plant kept unsprayed. With cymbidiums, *Odontoglossum* types etc., a centre leaf may turn brown and is easily removed without too much harm to the growth. However, if the outside leaves are also brown the rot has come from the base and the whole growth should be removed and the plant kept on the dry side until another new growth starts.

SPRAYING AND DRYNESS

Cool-growing orchids will want only an occasional spray on bright sunny days. Dry plants in dry surroundings for too long can develop a sticky residue on the underside of the leaves and on newly developing growths – mostly on cymbidiums, *Odontoglossum* types, coelogynes and encyclias. This is not quite the same as the sugary nectar which appears as a single droplet at the base of a bud, and should not be confused with the sticky substance secreted by greenfly. A droplet at the base of the bud is not harmful, but is a healthy sign and only needs to be removed if a mould is found to be growing upon it. The other stickiness should be wiped away, using a leaf wipe. Growing cases and converted aquaria can become too damp. It may become necessary to remove the plants for watering and return when they have drained.

INDEX

ACKNOWLEDGEMENTS

The publishers are grateful to the following agencies for granting permission to reproduce the following colour photographs: Photos Horticultural Picture Library (pp. 2/3, 7, 15, 21, 22, 25, 26, 27, 40, 41, 45, 47, 48, 49, 51, 52, 54, 57, 59, 60, 63, 75, 89, 105 & 113); the Harry Smith Horticultural Photographic Collection (pp. 7, 15, 59, 75, 89, 105 and 113). The following photographs were taken by Ed Gabriel: pp. 53, 64, 67, 69, 70, 73, 78, 81, 85, 92, 93, 100, 101, 102, 103, 106, 109 and 110. All the line drawings are by Brian Rittershausen.